My "I" Problem with God's Word

Daily Devotions 1-50

Rick Metrick, PhD

My "I" Problem with God's Word
by Rick Metrick, PhD

Printed in the United States of America

ISBN 9781615791385

Unless otherwise indicated, Bible quotations are from the King James Version 1611. Brackets, [ ], represents the author's addition and not part of the 1611.

www.xulonpress.com

Contents

Preface... ix

Chapter 1 **My "I" Problem with Being Thankful**
1 Thessalonians 5:18 11

Chapter 2 **My "I" Problem with Knowing My Need**
Philippians 4:19...23

Chapter 3 **My "I" Problem with Producing Good Works**
Ephesians 2:10...35

Chapter 4 **My "I" Problem with Spiritual Battles**
2 Corinthians 10:3-4.......................................47

Chapter 5 **My "I" Problem with Godly Thinking**
2 Corinthians 10:5 59

Chapter 6 **My "I" Problem with Being a Living Sacrifice**
Romans 12:1...71

Chapter 7 **My "I" Problem with Renewing My Mind**
Romans 12:2...83

Chapter 8 **My "I" Problem with My Faith Being Tested**
1 Peter 1:6-7 95

Chapter 9 **My "I" Problem with Not Loving the World**
1 John 2:15 107

Chapter 10 **My "I" Problem with Forgiving Others**
Matthew 6:14-15 119

Dedicated to

My loving wife, Karen, who has honored our Lord during a long season of trials: You are God's gift to me. "We are blessed more than we could ever deserve."

The congregation of Jones Memorial Baptist Church, my flock and my friends: Your support, love, and devotion to our Lord and his servants have made this book a reality.

JUST HONOR GOD!

Preface

God's ways are not our ways, neither are his thoughts our thoughts. It should come as no surprise that the teachings found in his book, the Bible, often conflict with our thoughts and behaviors. This conflict sets the stage for **My "I" Problem with God's Word.** These devotions, written in the first person, do not describe the author's personal struggles with God's Word (although, I see myself on every page). Rather, the reader is to become the "I." This allows you not only to enter into the struggle, but also the victory found in God's Word.

Each chapter highlights one or two verses, uniquely explained and applied through five daily readings. I would suggest you spend the week memorizing these Scriptures. Hiding the Word in your heart is the key to avoid sinning against God. Each daily reading ends with a **Search Me, O God** section, which includes discussion suggestions, questions, and challenging comments, appropriate for your personal quiet time or group discussion. You may also find it helpful to jot a few personal comments in this section. The readings conclude with a **Thought for the Day**, a quote from that day's reading. Take a few moments at the end of each devotional to meditate on the daily thought before ending with prayer.

May these simple ramblings assist you in conforming to God's will for your life. Welcome to **My "I" Problem with God's Word**.

Rick

Chapter 1

My "I" Problem
With Always
Being Thankful

Day 1   "In Everything"

Day 2   "Give Thanks"

Day 3   "This is the Will of God"

Day 4   "Concerning You"

Day 5   "In Christ Jesus"

*"In every thing give thanks;
for this is the will of God
in Christ Jesus concerning you"
(1 Thessalonians 5:18)*

My "I" Problem with Always Being Thankful "In Everything"
Day 1
"In every thing give thanks;
for this is the will of God
in Christ Jesus concerning you"
(1 Thessalonians 5:18)

Being thankful is not an easy virtue, though my blessings far outweigh what I deserve. I count every breath, hug, relationship, and joy a blessing. Yet, if thankfulness only embraces the pleasant things of life, it would be rather easy. Yet, that brand of gratitude is not Christian at all; it is far more self-honoring than God-honoring. Godly appreciation goes well beyond good times, which is no easy task, and embraces the overwhelming challenges of crisis, difficulties, struggles, and demonic attacks.

However, God is about to expand my thankfulness into the potentially dark, dreadful world of *"every thing."* I freely confess I regularly struggle with the *"every thing(s)"* of life. Many *"every thing(s)"* challenge my sense of right and wrong, greet me with pain, leave me disillusioned, and cast doubt on the very faith I claim to embrace. To be thankful for *"every thing"* is neither easy nor natural. These are times when God takes me beyond myself. Father, open my heart to the apostle's words and massage them into my inner self. May thanksgiving be the trademark of my life. Amen.

"In every thing give thanks." My calling, my destiny, my privilege is to face every joy, sorrow, blessing, and obstacle with the complete confidence and comfort that *"this is the will of God in Christ Jesus."* In doing so, I often find myself challenged to embrace some very unpleasant experiences with the spiritual perception of one who receives them as gifts from my heavenly Father.

"Give thanks." It is often difficult to see unrelenting obstacles and unfriendly struggles as gifts from God. Not only must I see them as heaven-sent or heaven-allowed gifts, I must do so with a deep sense of thankfulness. At best, this is a challenging mission; at worst, it seems nearly impossible. However, God's Word always gives meaning, imparts strength, introduces wisdom, and offers hope. Armed with this confidence, I begin the journey of finding meaning, strength and hope in Paul's challenging words. Father, I sit at your holy footstool waiting to be instructed by the Holy One, cleansed of all sin, and transported into spiritual maturity.

Thought for the Day: My calling, my destiny, my privilege is to face every joy, sorrow, blessing, and obstacle with the complete confidence and comfort that *"this is the will of God in Christ Jesus."*

<u>Search Me, O God!</u>

- Do you agree that being thankful only in good times is not a Christian virtue? Explain.

- What are Satan's attacks against you doing to your attitude of thanks?

- Difficulties dispute our sense of justice, inflict pain, make us cynical, and cast doubt on our faith. Explain how your trials affect your Christian walk.

- What gives you joy and assurance in the face of difficult obstacles?

- We must see troubles as heaven-sent or heaven-allowed gifts. In what ways do you show thankfulness to God?

- How would your life change with this as your life's mission?

My "I" Problem with Always Being Thankful
"Give Thanks"
Day 2
"In every thing give thanks;
for this is the will of God
in Christ Jesus concerning you"
(1 Thessalonians 5:18)

"Give thanks." On the surface, these words seem familiar friends. Praising God, offering thanks, and living with gratitude are hallmarks of the faith. Appreciation is at the heart of worship. Some lift their hands; many shout; and others bow in silence. However, these two words invite me to a level of spirituality few ever attain. Not only do they require I see my difficult, sometimes tragic, circumstances as gifts from God, they demand I refrain from my natural bent towards negativism, depression, criticism, anxiety, and self-pity. It is no easy task to be thankful in a thankless situation. Yet, God has blessed me too much not to *"give thanks."* Supernatural praise begins with a Father-knows-best mindset, moving me to embrace *"every thing"* as Christ did the cross.

"In every thing." If not for the preposition *"in,"* the exchange would be too great, if not impossible. How horrible it would be if the Spirit chose "for" instead. How unreasonable God would be to require thankfulness for chronic pain, tragic deaths, or financial collapse. Somehow, being thankful *"in"* the crisis seems more attainable. Unexpectedly, *"in"* creates a vast distance between my crisis and me. Crisis overwhelms inviting self-focus to prowl as an unseen predator of my soul. *"In"* is a magnet drawing me close to God, disconnecting me from the problem and reconnecting me with the heavenly Problem-Solver. I raise my hand in praise for a little preposition.

"In." At times, I find myself *"in"* some very difficult situations. Sitting by the bed of a dying friend, looking in the eyes of a grieving husband, witnessing the devastation left behind by a natural disaster, or watching the horror of a broken relationship remind me of the deep pools of human tragedy, which often rob me of joy. The sobering reality is that life is difficult, unfair, and regularly takes us to the breaking point. God's Spirit, however, elevates me beyond these obstacles into the presence of the Lord, where there is unspeakable joy. When the struggles of life leave me in the mire of despair, I will find my comfort and strength in the presence of my Lord.

Thought for the Day: The sobering reality is that life is difficult, unfair, and regularly takes us to the breaking point. God's Spirit, however, elevates me beyond these obstacles into the presence of the Lord, where there is unspeakable joy.

<u>Search Me, O God!</u>

- What is the danger of viewing worship as an action instead of a relationship?

- What do you think about the phrase "thankful in a thankless situation?

- What does your response to hard times say about your concept of God?

- How would the word "for" change the meaning of this phrase?

- The purpose of problems is to draw us closer to the Problem-Solver. Do you think most give the problem more attention and than the Solver?

- Think of times when God has given you joy and peace in the darkest moment of trials.

My "I" Problem with Always Being Thankful
"The Will of God"
Day 3
"In every thing give thanks;
for this is the will of God
in Christ Jesus concerning you"
(1 Thessalonians 5:18)

"For." Though God does not always explain his actions or his commands, he is about to step out of character, bring me into his confidence, and reveal the reason he is insistent that I develop the heavenly habit of thankfulness. Though there is much more to say about it, the ultimate reason that I am to be thankful is *"for this is the will of God."* This is God's utmost desire for my life. It is what makes God happy and is in the best interest of his children. I am shocked that God would take the time to bring me in to his wonderful confidence. I am thankful that he has clearly told me what I can do to please him. In addition, I am humbled that he would take a personal interest in my life. God concentrates the secret to pleasing him and receiving his best in the simple attitude of gratitude. Father, you know that I long to please you and to experience your will in my life. May you receive honor as I pursue your utmost desire for my life.

"This is the will of God." Many exercise great effort and devote inordinate amounts of time, energy, and contemplation seeking God's will without realizing that with few exceptions, it is already before them. In failing to see my current situations as God's will for my life, I quickly become disgruntled and preoccupied with "something" that may not exist. The result is predictable: I pray for my *"every thing"* to end, loath its interruption, frantically attempt to escape its grip, pity my misfortune, and angrily despise its existence. I wrongfully imagine that if the *"every thing(s)"* of temptations, difficulties, trials, and discomforts suddenly vanished I would be more able to offer God *"thanks."* In the end, I disregard the example of Jesus at Gethsemane: *"the cup which my Father hath given me, shall I not drink it?" (John 18:11b).*

"The will of God." To discard God's will is to discard God. With every encounter and at every turn, God's plan is ever before me. It is God's here-and-now will, which I must embrace, not the yet-to-be. In fact, I am convinced that God may never reveal his yet-to-be will if I fail to embrace him and his here-and-now will. As difficult as it is to accept, I know my present circumstances are part of God's plan for my life.

Thought for the Day: It is God's here-and-now will, which I must embrace, not the yet-to-be. I know my present circumstances are part of God's plan for my life.

<u>Search Me, O God!</u>

- What might be the reason God generally does not tell us why or even what he is doing?

- Thankfulness is God's will for our lives. By this standard, what do you need to change in order to be in the center of his will?

- Many seek to know God's specific will for their lives without being obedient to his revealed will. How might this effect their spiritual growth?

- What is the risk of being preoccupied with your trials and troubles?

- What do you think about the statement "To discard God's will is to discard God"?

- What is God's here-and-now will for your life?

- Meditate often on this, because it goes completely against our natural self.

My "I" Problem with Always Being Thankful
"Concerning You"
Day 4
"In every thing give thanks;
for this is the will of God
in Christ Jesus concerning you"
(1 Thessalonians 5:18)

"Concerning you." Seldom does God grace me with an explanation why unpleasant *"every thing*(s)*"* happen. He simply gives them, one-by-one, with a single objective, which Paul calls *"concerning you."* In other words, he carefully considers my life and determines exactly what is in my best interest. It is not for me to determine what I want, but to accept what God gives. I have no business dwelling on what could have been if only things might have been different. Such speculation can only lead to one conclusion: I would have been outside God's will. I might have a less disruptive, more sanitized life; but I would have missed *"the will of God."* If I am to overcome my spiritual "I" problem, living outside the will of God is never a viable option. To think such thoughts invites Satan's four-fold assault of resentment, bitterness, anxiety, and self-pity.

"Concerning you." I must embrace *"every thing,"* pleasant or unpleasant, as *"the will of God in Christ Jesus concerning."* This is such a strenuous task that I find it imperative to meditate often on *Jeremiah 29:11* — *"For I know the thoughts that I think toward you, saith the LORD, thoughts of peace, and not of evil, to give you an expected end."* I am humbled that God considers my life and tailor makes a unique prescription just for me. Thank you, Lord, that when you think about me, you have *"thoughts of peace, and not of evil."*

"This." Now, it is important to note that *"the will of God"* involves two matters. The first is the actual event and the second is my attitude. It is not only God's will for me to receive whatever he dispenses; I must express genuine gratitude while experiencing God's tailor-made trials for my life. In the first instance, the actual event, I am without the slightest control. Many trials, from mild irritants to soul wrenching, are unwelcomed intruders that I have to endure. However, my response is entirely up to me. I must never forget that whatever *"this"* hardship may be, it is God's sovereign and perfect design for my life. I can choose the lower ground and become problem-focused, which leads to bitterness, self-pity, criticism, and confusion or I can cling to God's higher ground and *"give thanks."* When I embrace *"this,"* I embrace God.

Thought for the Day: I must embrace *"every thing,"* pleasant or unpleasant, as *"the will of God in Christ Jesus concerning"* my life.

<u>Search Me, O God!</u>

- What is happening in your life right now is part of God's best for your life. How difficult is it to accept?

- If you are seeking to honor God with your life, it is important to remember that any other circumstance than what you are experiencing would place you outside God's will.

- Do you have a difficult time accepting that trials are part of God's will?

- How easy is it to overlook the gratitude part of God's will for your life?

- Do you embrace the lower ground of problem-focus or higher ground of thanksgiving?

- This is the path to intimacy with God.

My "I" Problem with Always Being Thankful
"In Christ Jesus"
Day 5

"In every thing give thanks;
for this is the will of God
in Christ Jesus concerning you"
(1 Thessalonians 5:18)

"Thanks." Thank God my difficult, and in some cases, backbreaking experiences are all part of his divine will for my life. If I am certain that *"this is the will of God in Christ Jesus concerning"* me, I can enter into the Psalmist's invitation, *"Let us come before his presence with thanksgiving" (Psalm 95:2a)*. However, if doubt enters, I stand before God consumed with rage, frustration, and self-justification. When I question why, I miss the point all together. Logic will not get me through my troubles and explanations will not increase my faith. The exercise of gratitude alone will keep my soul secure, my mind pure, and my spirit focused on his sacred program for my life. An attitude of gratitude is not something I put on and off as needed, it is the garment of my soul and the fabric of my spirit-centered life. Otherwise, any attempt at thankfulness will result in inauthenticity, emptiness, or bitterness.

"In Christ Jesus." The mention of his official title (*"Christ,"* the Anointed One) and his earthly name (*"Jesus"*) are intentionally given and strategically placed to reinforce this heavenly perspective of God's will. Because I am *"in Christ" (2 Corinthians 5:17)*, I am not only the object of God's affection, but the target of Satan's attacks. *"Jesus"* put it this way, *"If ye were of the world, the world would love his own: but because ye are not of the world, but I have chosen you out of the world, therefore the world hateth you" (John 15:19)*. However, it is also because I am *"in Christ"* that each devilish attack becomes a part of God's marvelous plan for my life. The book of *Job* clearly reveals that Satan exercises no more interference than God permits. Joseph's explained, *"But as for you, ye thought evil against me; but God meant it unto good" (Genesis 50:20a)*. Hell's interference is not beyond God's transforming power to reshape into *"the will of God in Christ Jesus concerning"* me.

These are words of survival from Heaven as I journey through a life of hardships on earth. I can find renewed strength, endurance, and gratitude in the face of *"every thing"* that comes my way.

Thought for the Day: Each devilish attack becomes a part of God's marvelous plan for my life. No interference from Hell is beyond God's transforming power to reshape it into *"the will of God in Christ Jesus concerning"* me.

<u>Search Me, O God!</u>

- Does knowing God is accomplishing his will in your life add to your spirit of worship?

- Does knowing why God is doing what he is doing really help us endure the trial with thankfulness?

- True thanksgiving is a lifestyle and not an occasional holy expression.

- What does it mean to be *"in Christ"*?

- Do you believe believers understand the implications of living in a world that hates them?

- Have you seen God transform Satan's attacks into a wonderful way of meeting his will for your life?

- What are your biblical "words of survival"?

- Reflect on these words. You will need them often.

Chapter 2

My "I" Problem
With Knowing
What I Need

Day 6   "God"

Day 7   "But My God Shall"

Day 8   "All Your Need"

Day 9   "His Riches In Glory In Christ"

Day 10   "Supply All Your Need"

*"But my God shall supply all your need
according to his riches in glory
in Christ Jesus"
(Philippians 4:19)*

My "I" Problem with Knowing What I Need
"God"
Day 6
"But my God shall supply all your need
according to his riches in glory
in Christ Jesus"
(Philippians 4:19)

Daily I encounter many opportunities to redefine my *"need"* list. I find it rather easy to elevate things formerly considered luxuries to the status of *"need."* Every new invention, amazing innovation, or recent advancement tantalizes my insatiable appetite for more. My fascination with materialism is inexcusable and embarrassing. As I am *"increased with goods,"* I quickly become defensive of my self-indulgent ways. Compared with a believer's *"need"* list from a century ago, mine suddenly seems indulgent, extravagant, and trivial. I doubt Paul's original audience (impoverished slaves struggling to survive Rome's Jesus-hating vice-like grip) received *Philippians 4:19* with the same arrogance and excess I have. May God rescue me from my wants-addiction and reveal to me my real *"need."*

"But my God." I am often humbled and deeply convicted when I consider the simple words *"but my God."* They demand practical faith, which I find far more challenging than a simple declaration of belief in God. Of course, I believe in him, but counting on God to meet my needs isn't as easy as it might seem. The painfully authentic reason for my lack of faith in God is the excessive amount of faith I still have in myself. I simply believe that with enough calculation and planning, I can meet my own needs. So, other than an obligatory quick, not to mention, insincere prayer, I ask God for help and proceed to lay him aside, living the life of a practical atheist (believing, yet not believing). Surely, I can understand the seeker's dilemma when he cried out, *"Lord, I believe, help thou my unbelief" (Mark 9:24b)*. These words encourage me as well, for they acknowledge a certain degree of faith and the promise of greater faith to come.

"My God." The lack of attention God receives from churchgoers is disheartening. My natural tendency is to receive from him without taking time to *"know him" (Philippians 3:10)*. Even the devils believe in God. To some, he is *"God";* to others, he is *"my God."* The difference separates those who believe in his existence from those who trust him with their lives.

Thought for the Day: The painfully authentic reason for my lack of faith in God is the excessive amount of faith I still have in myself.

Search Me, O God!

- In your opinion, how materialistic is the average 21st century Christian?

- How might a modern day s need list differ from one of the 1st century?

- A God worth believing in is a God worth _____.

- In the context of this paragraph, what do you think of the phrase "practical atheist"?

- Saving faith is seed faith. Authentic seed faith will bear the fruit of faith—confidence in God.

- What is the difference between knowing God and knowing about God?

My "I" Problem with Knowing What I Need
"But My God Shall"
Day 7
"But my God shall supply all your need
according to his riches in glory
in Christ Jesus"
(Philippians 4:19)

*"**But**."* My mind is analytical and constantly searches for answers, solutions, and creative responses to satisfy what I call my needs. It's no surprise, then, that such mind games only lead to sleepless nights, irritable moods, and the terrible feeling of helplessness; except on those few occasions when I have been able, or so it seemed, to figure the whole thing out. The pride that results from such a discovery is all I need to continue my vain attempt at meeting my own needs. This is the reason the Holy Spirit often interrupts my life with the powerful word *"but."* He did the same thing when Jonah intended to meet his needs apart from God. God responded to his *"but Jonah" (Jonah 1:3a)* with a resounding *"but the Lord" (Jonah 1:4a).*

"But." Thank God for the little word *"but."* In it, I see the pursuing love of God in providing for my life's need. Lord, for the moment and I pray for the rest of my life, I renounce my need to fix and figure, and release it all into your holy care.

"But my God shall." I must make my stand against all the difficulties and impossibilities of life in these words—'*but my God shall."* He *"shall"* provide, without doubt. *"Shall"* leaves no room for exceptions. My God will always do what he promises. Thank God, he interrupts circumstances and difficulties to accomplish his overall will for my life.

"My God shall." I will never attain unwavering confidence unless my relationship with God is intimate enough that I may call him *"my God."* This is more than an intellectual understanding of God, and it is much more than a declaration of devotion to him. Some might have a superficial relationship with the one they call *"God."* Others may have progressed to the "our *God"* level of commitment. However, it is only in experiencing the personal intimacy of the *"my God"* relationship that I draw the confident assurance I can trust him, I can wait on him, and I can rest patiently in him. He becomes *"my God"* as I face the daily grind, as I cling to him during trials, and as I embrace him through temptation. I am stunned by the intimacy Jesus had with the Father, leading him to cry out from the cross, *"My God, my God."* How I long for such oneness with the Father.

Thought for the Day: I must make my stand against all the difficulties and impossibilities of life in these words—'*but my God shall.*" He *"shall"* provide, without doubt. *"Shall"* leaves no room for exceptions.

<u>Search Me, O God!</u>

- The risk of living without God-dependency is the hardness that results from being able to meet some of your own needs.

- Can you remember times when the Holy Spirit interrupted your life with a "but"?

- Enter every trial, every circumstance with the total confidence that "God shall."

- What does it take to develop a "my God" relationship? How would you describe it?

- How tender Jesus' emotions were toward his Father at his greatest moment of agony. May I do the same.

- How confident are you that God keeps his promises?

My "I" Problem with Knowing What I Need
"All Your Need"
Day 8
"But my God shall supply all your need
according to his riches in glory
in Christ Jesus"
(Philippians 4:19)

"Your need." A major area of contention between the Spirit of God and my own spirit lies in agreeing on what my actual needs are. At times, I wonder why he does not see my needs as I see them. Why does God not heal a faithful saint, reconcile a wounded marriage, or prosper those who honor him? This whole *"need"* issue is as disturbing as it is confusing. I trust him, but I do not begin to understand him. Yet, what good is a God that I can understand? By faith, I believe Father knows best.

"Need." I not only have an innate sense of responsibility to provide for my needs, but I also possess an arrogant confidence that I nearly always know what I need. This is true in finances, relationships, trials, desires, and much more. I am intrigued and somewhat insulted that God summarizes my complicated life with a diminutive *"need."* At least he could have added an "s" on the end! I have needs, many needs. Why would he minimize my needs with a solitary *"need"*? I feel so unimportant, so under appreciated. Does God not understand how overwhelming life can be? Yet, I cannot deny that all my needs are nothing compared to the all-sufficient one. If he sees my complicated life as a singular *"need,"* then it is certain he is neither overwhelmed nor outmatched by those things that baffle or immobilize me.

"Need." *"Need"* refers to necessity, the bottom-line condition. It appears that one *"need"* far out weighs all other needs and is the foundation upon which every other need is satisfied. It would appear that a financial crisis, difficult relationship, major decision, or weakness ought to drive me back to an ultimate singular *"need"* that God alone can meet. Therefore, I wonder, "What is the ultimate need in any Christian's life?" Jesus seems to have summarized it in *Matthew 4:4* when he announced to Satan, *"It is written, Man shall not live by bread alone, but by every word that proceedeth out of the mouth of God."* Beyond hunger and thirst, Jesus' greatest need was guidance from his Father's Word. I humbly consent that my *"need"* for Wisdom's direction far outweighs any other. There, I find strength, meaning, fulfillment, understanding, faith, hope, and God himself.

Thought for the Day: He sees my complicated life as a singular *"need"* and is neither overwhelmed nor outmatched by those things that baffle or immobilize me.

<u>Search Me, O God!</u>

- How do you answer these questions?

- It is not necessary to understand God in order to know that his ways are true and righteous.

- Have you ever felt this way?

- Can I get an Amen?

- Before reading on, what do you suppose is "the ultimate need in any Christian's life"?

- May your spirituality develop to the point that God's Word brings you ultimate satisfaction and nourishment.

- Live by this!

My "I" Problem with Knowing What I Need
"His Riches In Glory In Christ"
Day 9
"But my God shall supply all your need
according to his riches in glory
in Christ Jesus"
(Philippians 4:19)

"Jesus." His situation was desperate and his needs were obvious. *"Jesus"* had fasted 40 days in the wilderness and required immediate nourishment, or he would die. In keeping with his evil nature, Satan, the Tempter, entered the scene at the time of his greatest need with a solution, *"If thou be the Son of God, command that these stones be made bread" (Matthew 4:3).* Makes sense to me. What possible need could be greater at this crucial moment in our Lord's life? Yet, Jesus' reply both amazes and humbles me, *"It is written, Man shall not live by bread alone, but by every word that proceedeth out of the mouth of God."*

"Need ... Jesus." I don't get it. Is Jesus saying that his immediate need wasn't physical at all? Is he revealing that the one thing I need for survival is mystical, spiritual, and eternal? I think so. My greatest need, as a child of God, was his greatest need. This *"need"* is completely satisfied *"by every word that proceedeth out of the mouth of God."* I am ashamed at how often I exchange Truth for a practical common sense antidote for life's challenges. Lord, keep me hungering and thirsting after righteousness.

"His riches." Behind the revealed Word of God, the Bible is the immeasurable wealth of God's person. He is infinitely rich in wisdom, abounding in love and overflowing with mercy. His grace is limitless, as is his kindness, goodness, faithfulness, and resourcefulness. Solomon's glory was a single grain of sand on an endless shoreline of God's magnificent wealth.

"Your Need ... His riches." God has reserved everything I could ever need through his endless resources. This is a difficult spiritual principle to live because I naturally lean on my own ingenuity. Often, I find that in order to follow through on my resources I must dismiss God's resources as insufficient. Such is the arrogance of a man who leans on his own understanding.

"According to his riches." Every need, every challenge, every difficulty must drive me to one place, and one place only, the *"riches"* of

the Word of God. I must sit silently before his Word. Now, this does not deny God's direct intervention and willingness to meet a health need, emotional need, or employment need. Many times, he has provided in wondrous and undeserved ways.

Thought for the Day: Every need, challenge, and difficulty must drive me to the *"riches"* of the Word.

Search Me, O God!

- Satan is the master deceiver, causing us to confuse our priorities.

- Is Jesus implying that food is unnecessary? Or is he implying a comparison perspective?

- Spiritual growth demands total dependency on God. What does that mean? How does that look? How is it attained?

- Sitting before the Word of God when everything inside you says act, is a step of faith and reliance on God.

- God's Word is the place of comfort and solace. How has the Word comforted or strengthened you throughout life?

My "I" Problem with Knowing What I Need
"Supply All Your Need"
Day 10
"But my God shall supply all your need
according to his riches in glory
in Christ Jesus"
(Philippians 4:19)

"According to his riches." The emphasis in this passage is a deeper singular need, which I believe is satisfied in reading, meditating, and memorizing God's Word. Lord, during these difficult days, may I give greater attention to my relationship with you than I do the resolution of my problems. Keep my thoughts on you and your Word in me. I will dwell on it as my morning and evening sacrifice; I will hide it in my heart that I might avoid the lure of sin; I will meditate on it that I might be purified; and I will seek it that I might know your for my life.

"Supply all . . . in Christ Jesus." Furthermore, my God is intent on supplying *"all"* my need. His work is full and complete, bringing wholeness and wellness to my otherwise destitute soul. He does this *"through Christ Jesus."* Jesus is the executor of the Father's riches and distributes them fully to me: *"Now they have known that all things whatsoever thou hast given me are of thee. For I have given unto them the words which thou gavest me; and they have received them." (John 17:7,8a).*

"All." *"All"* that God has for me will be delivered to me *"through Christ Jesus."* God's provision offers unparalleled comfort and courage! Since he supplies all, I have need of nothing. Through Christ's provision, worry melts away, trials lose their stronghold, and obstacles dissolve.

"Glory." Now, on a lower but much needed level, the practical side of my neediness is this: every response of God to my needs comes out of and from his own *"glory."* The phrase, *"his riches in glory,"* finds its parallel in the writings of James, *"Every good gift and every perfect gift is from above, and cometh down from the Father of lights, with whom is no variableness, neither shadow of turning" (James 1:17).* Every God-supplied gift originates in Heaven and is freely deposited *"through Christ Jesus."*

The precious promise of *Philippians 4:19* gives me rest from fear, replaces worry with peace, and extinguishes all anxieties. My God knows all I need and is more than ready to provide as he sees fit; and that is all I need. A singular *"need"* met by my Lord is sufficient provision for everything in life.

Thought for the Day: Since he supplies all, I have need of nothing. Through Christ's provision, worry melts away, trials lose their stronghold, and obstacles dissolve.

<u>Search Me, O God!</u>

- Memorizing the Word is not enough. Meditation drives truth deep into our spirits. Try this: Memorize, Meditate, Pray the verse you memorized, then apply it to your life.

- If I am intent on defining my need, I will not realize his full work. What I am experiencing is exactly what I "need" to experience. It is his provision. I must embrace it

- Compare this thought with Psalm 23: "I shall not want."

- Think about the implications of "every gift originates in Heaven."

- God's Word is the place of comfort and solace.

- Why do so many seem dissatisfied with God's provision?

Chapter 3

My "I" Problem
With Producing
Good Works

Day 11   "For We Are"

Day 12   "His Workmanship"

Day 13   "Created In Christ Jesus"

Day 14   "Unto Good Works"

Day 15   "That We Should Walk In Them"

"For we are his workmanship created in Christ Jesus unto good works, which God hath before ordained that we should walk in them"
(Ephesians 2:10)

My "I" Problem with Producing Good Works
"For We Are"
Day 11

*"For we are his workmanship created in Christ
Jesus unto good works, which God hath
before ordained that we should walk in them"
(Ephesians 2:10)*

What worthwhile thing could I ever do for God? Surely, my feeble effort at *"good works"* more closely resembles a toddler's attempt at rocket science than it does a child of God producing something of value for his heavenly Father. Many times, I have attempted to do something good for the Lord, yet personal gain and self-indulgence tainted my motives. As I turn my heart to *Ephesians 2:10,* I recognize my low expectations and heightened sense of inadequacy.

"For." Seldom does a verse stand alone on the pages of Scripture. Attempting to offer insight without the light of its immediate context is both dangerous and irresponsible. *"For"* invites me to discover and appreciate the foundation on which *Ephesians 2:10* rests. *Verses 8-9* are an exquisite couplet of verses describing the underserved generosity of God in saving me from my sins (*"for by grace are ye saved"*). God's unparalleled grace has redeemed me out of the darkness of sin and into the light of his glorious redemption. These verses remind me that belief in Jesus makes God's grace-gift possible. Now, this is where the passage really gets interesting. Amazingly, I was so desperately hopeless, that I was unable to produce saving faith (*"and that not of yourselves"*). On the day I received Christ as Savior, the first *"gift of God"* was not salvation; the first gift was believing faith. If it were not for Jesus giving me the ability to believe in him, I would have never believed. I did nothing to deserve salvation (including the exercise of faith in Jesus) and I have nothing to *"boast"* in now that I am saved. I leave these verses behind with conflicting feelings: overwhelmed by God's wonderful grace and haunted by my unworthiness. This is how Paul must have felt when he cried out, *"O wretched man that I am!"* (*Romans 7:24*). My self-worth has plummeted and my complete inability to serve God torments me.

"We are." I realize the importance of knowing who I am and what I am all about. Nevertheless, it is equally important that I recognize who I am not and what I am not all about. In the end, I am to be about my Father's business. *"He must increase, but I must decrease"* (*John 3:30*).

Thought for the Day: God's unparalleled grace has redeemed me out of the darkness of sin and into the light of his glorious redemption.

<u>Search Me, O God!</u>

- As a believer, is this a healthy attitude to have?

- How difficult is it for you to have pure motives when you serve the Lord?

- It is important not to take verses out of context.

- Have you accepted God's gift of eternal life?

- Is "grace" or "faith" the free gift in this verse?.

- Does your heart long to serve God? Answer only after much introspection and prayer.

- Do you believe we put too much emphasis on self-esteem or self-awareness?

- Take time to thank God for your salvation.

My "I" Problem with Producing Good Works
"His Workmanship"
Day 12
*"For we are his workmanship created in Christ
Jesus unto good works, which God hath
before ordained that we should walk in them"
(Ephesians 2:10)*

"We are." Everything I do or say originates out of self-belief—decisions made and unconsciously directing my every step. Two well-known verses reinforce this principle. The first is *Proverbs 23:7a* (*"For as he thinketh in his heart, so is he"*) and the second is *Matthew 12:34b* (*"out of the abundance of the heart the mouth speaketh"*). So, who am I? If I stop now, I regretfully have to conclude I am rather worthless for God— saved, but completely inept. I have spent my entire life longing to be of some use for my God. Yet, what I might count as useful seems terribly inadequate against the backdrop of God's bigger picture. I anxiously anticipate what follows.

"We are his." One glimpse at these words and I am immediately refreshed. I suddenly discover my actual identity. I belong to God and God alone! I am his! A few moments of reflection on this wonderful discovery, reminds me that my body has been transformed into *"the temple of the Holy Spirit"* (*1 Corinthians 6:19*). *1 Corinthians 6* ends with the important reminder that I no longer belong to myself and have been *"bought with a price,"* the blood of Jesus Christ. How blessed I am to be a child of the King, to call God my Father, Jesus my Savior, and the Spirit my guide. I have a renewed desire to honor him with this life. Armed with this new sense of identity, I can hardly wait to see what comes next.

"We are his workmanship." I am the handiwork of God. An artisan takes pride in his work and considers it an extension of himself. He takes raw materials and astounds us with his creation. If I am *"his workmanship,"* I also am an extension of the Heavenly Craftsman. The world will develop their impressions of God by observing my life. In fact, I am his walking testimonial. Therefore, it is imperative that my life gives others an accurate impression of who my Creator is and what he is all about. I no longer see myself as worthless. Rather, I am an expression of God's love, grace, and mercy. His holy presence shines through me. My worth, in Christ, is immeasurable. I am overwhelmed with praise and thanksgiving to God for my new identity in him—from worthless to worthy.

Thought for the Day: I suddenly discover my actual identity. I belong to God and God alone! I am his! I am an expression of God's love, grace, and mercy.

<u>Search Me, O God!</u>

- What is the difference between a believer and a nonbeliever's answer to the "Who am I" question?

- It is vital that we realize our insufficiency in order that Christ may be all-sufficient.

- Why is it important to remember that your body is the temple of God? What are the consequences of failing to remember this principle?

- What keeps your life from being an accurate impression of Christ?

- "Walk worthy of the vocation wherewith ye are called" (Ephesians 4:1)

- Our incredible worth is because of Christ's worthiness.

My "I" Problem with Producing Good Works
"Created in Christ Jesus"
Day 13

"For we are his workmanship created in Christ
Jesus unto good works, which God hath
before ordained that we should walk in them"
(Ephesians 2:10)

"His." It is rather embarrassing that I have spent so much time and energy thinking about my new worth, as though it were all about me. A moment of meditation on this possessive pronoun, *"His,"* reminds me that my worth is completely dependent on *"His"* worth. Everything revolves around my Lord, including my own life. It is a shame that I have often tried to make it the opposite—trying to convince God to revolve his existent around my situations and crisis. Instantly, I am elevated to a higher level of worship and my thoughts echo the heavenly adoration, *"Worthy is the Lamb."* Father, I praise you for all you do and who you are! Strengthen me against the ever-present lure of self-focus and immerse me into your wonderful self, to the end that *"for to me to live is Christ."*

"Created in Christ Jesus." This is not a reference to original creation— my physical self—but to the new birth, my spiritual self. Jesus has transformed me and I am a new creation (*2 Corinthians 5:17*). The word *"created"* is an interesting one. It refers to something made habitable or worth living in. Those who "flip houses" have a knack for turning shacks into mansions, and this is what *"Christ Jesus"* has done for me. He has taken this broken down, sin-infested, Hell bound soul and transformed it into *"a vessel unto honour, sanctified, and meet for the master's use, and prepared unto every good work."* (*2 Timothy 2:21*). *"Christ Jesus"* has entered my life and turned my vile body into his holy house. Incredibly, his dwelling place is in me. As for the tiny preposition *"in,"* it reminds me of my abiding place, my spiritual position, and my daily ambition. No longer *"dead in trespasses and sins"* (*Ephesians 2:1b*), I am alive *"in"* the body of Christ. May the Spirit ever remind me of this safe and glorious place to dwell; and may he warm my spirit with Jesus' call, *"Abide in me, and I in you"* (*John 15:4a*).

"Christ Jesus." This is the third mention of *"Christ Jesus."* *"Christ"* means "Anointed One." As a "Christian" I am an "anointed one"; anointed by the blood of Christ, the breath of the Spirit, and the adoption of the Father. May I live as one who has been anointed.

Thought for the Day: A moment of meditation on this possessive pronoun, *"His,"* reminds me that my worth is completely dependent on *"His"* worth.

<u>Search Me, O God!</u>

- When spiritual truth becomes a reality, let us avoid the Deceiver's attempt to turn the attention to ourselves instead of God.

- Our self-indulgent tendencies are great. Shine the light on Christ rather than yourself. Become God-indulgent!

- What changes has Christ made in you that are distinct from who you were without him?

- "In" is the position we have with Christ. What is the importance of knowing we are "in Christ"? What are the practical implications of being "in Christ"?

- What does the word "anointed" imply about our identity in Christ?

- The theme is "Yet, not I, but Christ."

My "I" Problem with Producing Good Works
"Unto Good Works"
Day 14

*"For we are his workmanship created in Christ
Jesus unto good works, which God hath
before ordained that we should walk in them"
(Ephesians 2:10)*

*"**U**nto good works."* In three simple words, I have found my life's direction, my purpose, and the holy legacy I am to leave behind. I cannot ignore the clarity of these words— *"unto good works."* My life must be completely devoted to honoring the Master through *"good works."* How trivial the word *"good"* has become. Often reserved for a child's behavior or a tasty bite of food, the Greek word for *"good"* is "agathos," a figure of speech describing the value and impact one life has on another. I suppose we are all born wanting to be significant to someone and to leave our thumbprint on them long after we leave this world behind. There can be no greater legacy to leave behind than the person of Jesus Christ in my life.

"Unto good works." Oh Lord, may I devote my life to drawing attention to you and downplaying me. Grant boldness to speak of you freely and often. May my *"good works"* grow thirty fold, sixty fold, and even a hundred fold *(Mark 4:20)* for your glory and honor. Though, *"in me (that is, in my flesh,) dwelleth no good thing" (Romans 7:18a)*, the blood of the Lamb has made me righteous. And, I rejoice, for God's goodness now dwells in me. This truth will never cease to astound me.

"Works." As I leave this phrase behind, I am reminded that *"works"* implies time and energy. Even the Greek word itself (ergon) shows the extraordinary amount of energy I am to exert in my efforts to produce any kind of *"good."* In a world full of evil, *"good works"* requires more energy than I, alone, am capable of generating, apart from the enabling power of the Spirit of God *("be strong in the Lord, and in the power of his might," Ephesians 6:10)*. Let me devote my energy, time, and resources to his mighty hand and for this mighty purpose. Let me daily receive strength from the power of his might.

"Workmanship ... Works." The Father has, through his Son, begun a good work in me—through Scripture, cleansing, conviction, experiences, and growth—that I might be prepared when the time comes for me to fulfill the task he places before me. All uneventful moments work together to prepare me for that crucial moment when

Jesus wants to touch a life through me. I am his *"workmanship"* and eternal is in the balance.

Thought for the Day: There can be no greater legacy to leave behind that the person of Jesus Christ in my life. Oh Lord, I devote my life to drawing attention to you.

<u>Search Me, O God!</u>

- Can you think of believers who leave the legacy of Christ behind?

- What are their characteristics of these believers?

- What prevents you from boldly living for Jesus?

- Is it true that living for Jesus is suppose to be difficult and require great amounts of energy?

- It is difficult and humbling to learn to be strong in Christ instead of ourselves.

- Consider how life events have prepared you for Christ's service.

- What legacy are you leaving behind?

My "I" Problem with Producing Good Works
"Than We Should Walk In Them"
Day 15

"For we are his workmanship created in Christ
Jesus unto good works, which God hath
before ordained that we should walk in them"
(Ephesians 2:10)

"Which God hath before ordained." Here is where my spiritual "I" problem collides with God's ultimate purpose for my life. I must remember, at all times, that God has *"ordained"* (designed, predetermined) me to actively live for him. If I decide otherwise, I lose my purpose and forfeit my destiny. What an extraordinary thought, especially when I understand its deeper spiritual, even mystical, meaning. It suggests that long before I existed, God called me to a life of *"good works."* In ages past, He determined that I am to have a vital roll in his kingdom. I am, without doubt, a man of destiny—destined to produce *"good works."* That is who I am; what I am all about; the very reason I exist. God has selected me to influence others for Jesus. The God I serve ordains where I am, who I am, and what I am to do for his glory. My response to any situation, any person, and any temptation, must be directed by the holy mission of producing good works to the glory of God. Everything becomes bearable and purposeful in light of this calling.

"That we should walk in them." My daily *"walk,"* my lifestyle, must accurately represent Jesus in every arena of life. I cannot afford to indulge in sinful self-interest or give Satan opportunity to quiet me. God did not save me to a life of bitterness, lust, or self-indulgence. The *"fruit of the Spirit"* must strongly influence every relationship, every decision, every action (*Galatians 5:22-23*). God has intended that love, joy, peace, longsuffering, gentleness, goodness, faith, meekness, and self-control become the moment-by-moment hallmarks of my life.

"In them." Because I am *"in Christ"* it is my joy, my duty, and my power to *"walk in"* *"good works."* Walking is a metaphor for the daily strides the moment-by-moment movements of life. "Good works" are not something I put on when I actively serve the Lord and take off when I am not. *"Good works"* are supposed to be the primary characteristic of every second of every day.

The message of *Ephesians 2:10* reminds me that God has created and strategically placed me where I am for one high and holy purpose, producing *"good works."*

44

Thought for the Day: I cannot afford to indulge in sin or give Satan opportunity to quiet me. God did not save me to a life of bitterness, lust, or self-indulgence.

<u>Search Me, O God!</u>

- Being ordained for a holy purpose gives us our ultimate objective.

- You were in his mind before he made the worlds. Is there anything that could offer us a greater identity?

- How important is it to be mindful of this purpose?

- How does your life line up to the "fruit of the spirit"?

- "Good works" must define every aspect of our lives.

- How will accepting this mission affect your life?

- Expect Satan to try everything to silence you. Don't give in. Let God speak through you!

Chapter 4

My "I" Problem
With Spiritual
Battles

Day 16   "We Walk in the Flesh"

Day 17   "We Do Not War After the Flesh"

Day 18   "The Weapons of our Warfare"

Day 19   "But Mighty Through God"

Day 20   "Pulling Down of Strongholds"

"For though we walk in the flesh, we do not war after the flesh: (For the weapons of our warfare are not carnal, but mighty through God to the pulling down of strong holds"
(2 Corinthians 10:3-4)

My "I" Problem with Producing Good Works
"We Walk in the Flesh"
Day 16

"For though we walk in the flesh, we do not war
after the flesh: (For the weapons of our warfare
are not carnal, but mighty through God to the
pulling down of strong holds"
(2 Corinthians 10:3-4)

Conflict is something I try to avoid. However, I have to admit that as my walk with God intensifies, so does my conflict with Hell. One spiritual skirmish after another seems to connect the days of my life. What is more, I grow weary of these frequent trials and relentless clashes. Lord, I freely confess my "I" problem with fighting spiritual battles. I sit at your feet longing for an empowering word for my life.

"We." Because I am a believer, God holds me to a higher standard than those outside the family. This is a sobering reminder when I am tempted to lust, unleash unedited verbal attacks, bask in self-pity, or embrace the twin demons of resentment and bitterness. I find some of God's "higher standards" more palatable than others. These offer precious promises and visions of a renewed Paradise just on the other side.

"For though we." However, the reality of the here-and-now sobers me with three simple words, *"For though we,"* making me brace for the impact. I have little doubt that the ensuing words will go against everything I naturally believe, feel, or do. O Father, will I react like many of the disciples in *John 6:60b*, who said, *"This is an hard saying; who can hear it?"* Or, will I be like the Emmaus disciples and exclaimed, *"Did not [my] heart burn within?"* Open my heart and burn your holy words into the inner recesses of my soul.

"We walk in the flesh." Depending on the context, at times *"flesh"* refers to my personal sin or sin nature, at other times it simply speaks of my earthly body. Here, Paul is saying, "We live in a body." Do I ever! Everyday I *"walk"* in a fleshly body full of aches and pains, surrounded by things I can touch, see, taste, hear, smell, and experience. Much of my life (*"walk"*)—an inordinate amount to be sure—is devoted to this fleshly body and the world in which it lives. Despite imperfections and shortcomings, I have taken quite a liking to my body. My aging skin loyally sticks with me through thick-and-thin. I could not imagine living one day without this fleshly companion. Now, the problem, of course, is that I quite often neglect, or forget all together, my spiritual self and the

invisible spirit world that surrounds me, living my life as a virtual nonbe-liever. It is disheartening how easily I reduce my life to aches, sniffles, work, recreation, and pleasure.

Thought for the Day: Because I am a believer, God holds me to a higher standard than those outside the family.

<u>Search Me, O God!</u>

- What type of spiritual conflicts do you encounter as you mature in Christ?

- God holds you to a higher standard and our responses are to honor him.

- Discuss the empowering of the Word of God in your life

- How do believers spend inordinate amounts of time on their physical selves?

- Does the average church prayer meeting spend too much time on health issues and too little on spiritual things?

My "I" Problem with Producing Good Works
"We Do Not War After The Flesh"
Day 17

"For though we walk in the flesh, we do not war
after the flesh: (For the weapons of our warfare
are not carnal, but mighty through God to the
pulling down of strong holds"
(2 Corinthians 10:3-4)

"We do not war after the flesh." My battle is not physical. I know this, but I do not always live it. Life is, at times, a struggle, even a tragedy. It would be quite easy to demonstrate that I <u>do</u> *"war after the flesh."* Every day, I face challenges, decisions, and struggles that awaken my natural senses. Yet, these words sober me and I, once again, become aware of the spiritual dimension of my life; there is more than meets the eye. My personal sin-style and numerous flaws are more than a defect in my genetic code or simply part of being human. So, why is it that I cannot consistently remember life is more than what I see? Paul was right, *"the flesh is weak."*

"War." In my youth, I struggled to justify bad things that happened to God's people. I was not only terribly disturbed when unfair trials knocked me off my feet; I was embarrassed. What would others think of a God who failed to protect his own? As years pass, my struggle finds rest in Jesus' sympathetic words, *"If ye were of the world, the world would love his own: but because ye are not of the world, but I have chosen you out of the world, therefore the world hateth you." (John 15:19)*. I am Hell's target and fully expect attacks from *"the fiery darts of the wicked" (Ephesians 6:16b)*. The troubles of life still bring me to my knees, but I accept them as an unavoidable and unrelenting part of my walk with Christ. Holy God, the *"war"* is long and hard; keep me strong.

"For the weapons of our warfare." *"Weapons"* and *"warfare"* are serious words. I am a warrior armed with deadly *"weapons,"* fighting an enemy whose intent is to *"sift [me] like wheat"* (a reality I dare not ignore). Paul reveals *"the weapons of our warfare"* in *Ephesians 6:14-18: "Stand therefore, having your loins girt about with truth, and having on the breastplate of righteousness; And your feet shod with the preparation of the gospel of peace; Above all, taking the shield of faith, wherewith ye shall be able to quench all the fiery darts of the wicked. And take the helmet of salvation, and the sword of the Spirit, which is the word of God: Praying always with all prayer and supplication in the*

Spirit, and watching thereunto with all perseverance and supplication for all saints." As a battle-ready saint, I wear a warrior's belt, breastplate, shoes, shield, helmet, and sword.

Thought for the Day: I am Hell's target and fully expect attacks from *"the fiery darts of the wicked" (Ephesians 6:16b).*

<u>Search Me, O God!</u>

- Ask the Holy Spirit to shine his searchlight on the inner recesses of your soul and reveal your personal sin-style.

- What makes it so difficult to remember life is more than what we see?

- Why does God allow us to experience unfair and relentless attacks from Hell? Why does God not stop them and give us peace on earth?

- What are your thoughts and how do you feel about being a spiritual warrior?

- Try to make some practical application to these weapons to your unique situations.

- Expectation requires preparedness.

My "I" Problem with Producing Good Works
"The Weapons of Our Warfare"
Day 18

*"For though we walk in the flesh, we do not war
after the flesh: (For the weapons of our warfare
are not carnal, but mighty through God to the
pulling down of strong holds"
(2 Corinthians 10:3-4)*

"Warfare." Warrior words bleed through the pages of Scripture. Since I am a soldier of Jesus Christ ready to fight a good fight against a wicked foe, why should I expect my life to be a calm, peaceful, tranquil exception to the rule? Peace is a casualty of war and conflict is its evil counterpart. There will always be trials, troubles, and tribulations, briefly separated by periodic cease-fires. As long as I live in enemy land, I can expect nothing less. My natural enemies include Satan, the world, and my own sin nature. In a highly calculated way, Satan unleashes his demonic army against me without warning. The world constantly arrays itself with opportunities to indulge in sin's pleasures. And, my flesh, full of ungodly desires and motives is always with me.

"Are not carnal." If the war were a physical one, God would have equipped me with physical weapons. However, since my war is against *"spiritual wickedness in high places,"* the weapons given me are neither *"carnal"* nor worldly. More often than not, I am tempted to fight the Enemy with things I can see, understand, and manipulate. It is natural to face financial needs, emotional issues, and innumerable problems with little or no regard to the supernatural quality of the conflict. How could my feeble strength, determination, resolve, resources, or intellect stand against the powers of Hell? To stand in the power of my might is certain defeat.

"Not carnal." However, there is more at stake than the obvious. I must see beyond the *"carnal"* (physical dimension) and into a dark, mystical world, where real battles are won or lost. The spiritual dimension is our greater reality.

"Not carnal." The girdle of truth secures me with God's non-negotiable absolutes. The breastplate of righteousness measures what is right by God's unqualified standards. The gospel of peace equips me with a non-anxious presence in the heat of battle. Faith is the ultimate shield against demonic attacks, while the helmet of salvation keeps my thoughts pure and true. Proper application of the Word destroys the power of temptation and creates divine strength. Intense prayer and spiritual alertness

remind me of the mystical implication of every crisis. I am well equipped. However, being equipped is not enough, unless I am trained to use the weapons of war against darkness.

Thought for the Day: How could my feeble strength, determination, resolve, resources, or intellect stand against the powers of Hell?

<u>Search Me, O God!</u>

- Why do we expect to have peace (the absence of conflict) when we live on a spiritual battle field?

- How does Satan use these three forces against you?

- Consider the spiritual warfare of believers in light of Job's story. What should be our expectations? Our preparation? Our concentration?

- How do we properly apply the Word to make us effective warriors for the Lord? What do you consider the more important verses/spiritual concepts to apply?

- There is no substitute for the power of God's might to battle Hell.

My "I" Problem with Producing Good Works
"But Mighty Through God"
Day 19

"For though we walk in the flesh, we do not war
after the flesh: (For the weapons of our warfare
are not carnal, but mighty through God to the
pulling down of strong holds"
(2 Corinthians 10:3-4)

"But mighty through God." These words expose the utter weakness I so desperately try to conceal, leaving me incompetent, vulnerable, and powerless. Oddly, this is exactly where God wants me. It is only in my weakness that God reveals his strength. Through out life, God has been convincing me of my spiritual Achilles' heel. Some might think that being aware of personal limitations would make me feel exposed, paranoid, and timid. However, the opposite has been my reality. When I am conscious of my weakness, I am forced to depend even more on the strengthening power of my God. Father, I no longer want to walk in my strength, but in the power of your holy might. Break me of self-dependency and shape me into Holy Spirit dependency. Amen

"Through God." Truth, righteousness, peace, faith, salvation, the Word, prayer, and watchfulness are too *"mighty"* to place in my feeble hands. Left to my care, they would be as useless as cars without gasoline, or computers without electricity. They are only *"mighty through God,"* which is how I need to live every day—deeply and desperately dependent on God. God alone empowers these weapons for battle. Taking hold of the gift given without clinging to the Gift-Giver is an inescapable prescription for failure.

"To the pulling down of strong holds." *"Pulling down,"* "kathairesis" is a very graphic word in the Greek language and can easily be translated "annihilation, devastation, or destruction." Spiritual *"weapons,"* when empowered by God, are capable of obliterating the Enemy's fortress, which Scripture calls *"strong holds."* Originally, a *"strong hold"* referred to an impenetrable military fortress, such as a castle. Figuratively, *"strong holds"* were the convincing arguments one might use to defend their position during a heated debate. Spiritually, *"strong holds"* are more than Satan's constant attacks against my physical world (similar to what happened to Job), they are demonic attempts to reprogram my mind. My mind is the battlefield and truth, righteousness, peace, faith, salvation, the Word, prayer, and watchfulness fortify me with power to

overcome Satan's hellish influence. May I keep my heart and mind on Christ Jesus.

Thought for the Day: When I am conscious of my weakness, I am forced to depend even more on the strengthening power of my God.

<u>Search Me, O God!</u>

- God only displays his strength in our weakness. Why does God not chose to display his strength through our strength?

- Our weak flesh takes things at face value. What's so bad about taking life at face value?

- The Holy Spirit empowered Jesus as he came out of the wilderness, and he will do the same for us when we step out of our wilderness adventure and into his strength.

- Our minds have become a massive battlefield in this spiritual clash. As a result, it is imperative that we renew our minds daily. How is mental renewing accomplished?

- Coming to the end of your rope has the promise of the blessing of strength.

- Expectation requires preparedness.

My "I" Problem with Producing Good Works
"The Pulling Down of Strongholds"
Day 20

"For though we walk in the flesh, we do not war
after the flesh: (For the weapons of our warfare
are not carnal, but mighty through God to the
pulling down of strong holds"
(2 Corinthians 10:3-4)

"Strong holds." I think of times I have set my heart on holy living, never once giving Satan a second thought. Because I did not appreciate the gravity of the matter, it was only a matter of time before I submitted to his relentless assault, abandoning holy living altogether. Satan's chronic assault on my spirit, mind, soul, possessions, and relationships has left me imprisoned by *"the lust of the flesh,"* intoxicated with *"the lust of the eyes,"* and infatuated with *"the pride of life."* However, there have also been times when I stood courageously against Satan's fiery darts, empowered by *"his might."* Those are times when, by the Spirit's inexhaustible power, I refused to deny the faith or compromise the truth.

"Strong holds." There are many kinds of satanic *"strong holds."* The Enemy is forever attacking me in a variety of creative ways. One of his most effective attacks are Compulsive Strongholds, which entice me day-by-day with an assortment of addictions, sexual perversions, and hard-heartedness. A second category I often encounter might be called Emotional Strongholds, which threaten me with immobilizing fears, uncontrollable rage, debilitating depression, and indescribable bitterness. Mental Strongholds are another form of *"strongholds"* Satan uses to fill my mind with godless philosophies, unholy influences, and ungodly friendships. Finally, I am rather familiar with Material Strongholds, which fascinate me with wealth, materialism, and immediate gratification. Thank God, these *"strong holds"* will not have the final word in my life.

2 Corinthians 10:3 brings me to a higher reality than I naturally experience. My struggles exceed simple problems, enticements, or trials. I clash every day with the spirit world and am well equipped to survive the most devilish attacks *"through God."* Victory is mine!

I can hardly wait for the Spirit's insight into the next verse, which will surely expand my understanding of this mighty spiritual struggle. *"Casting down imaginations, and every high thing that exalteth itself against the knowledge of God, and bringing into captivity every thought to the obedience of Christ." (verse 4).*

Thought for the Day: I clash every day with the spirit world and am well equipped to survive the most devilish attacks *"through God."*

<u>Search Me, O God!</u>

- Any commitment we make to God is an insult to Satan and an invitation for him to wreak havoc in our lives.

- We can only successfully stand against Satan through the Spirit.

- Does Satan have a Compulsive Stronghold in you?

- Does Satan have an Emotional Stronghold in you?

- Does Satan have a Mental Stronghold in you?

- Does Satan have a Materialistic Stronghold in you?

- We must be aware every day of Satan's attacks.

- We would be wise to walk in this truth.

Chapter 5

My "I" Problem
With Godly
Thinking

Day 21   "Casting Down Imaginations"

Day 22   "Casting Down...Every High Thing"

Day 23   "Every High Thing"

Day 24   "Exalteth Itself Against ... God"

Day 25   "Every thought to the Obedience"

"Casting down imaginations, and every high thing that exalteth itself against the knowledge of God, and bringing into captivity every thought to the obedience of Christ"
(2 Corinthians 10:5)

My "I" Problem with Godly Thinking
"Casting Down Imaginations"
Day 21

*"Casting down imaginations, and every high
thing that exalteth itself against the knowledge of
God, and bringing into captivity every thought
to the obedience of Christ"
(2 Corinthians 10:5)*

My thought life is my secret place. No one knows my late night worries, my early morning fears, my ungodly fantasies, or my secret wishes. A war of thoughts rages in my mind, often leaving me consumed with guilt, doubt, and confusion. These thoughts are so intrusive, so unpredictable, so enticing, and so unlike the true, honest, just, pure, lovely, and good report thoughts Paul lists in *Philippians 4:8*. I must admit that these thoughts are not always intrusive; sometimes I willfully welcome them, even invite them. I have a serious "I" problem with thinking godly thoughts.

"Imaginations." As long as I wear the armor of God, no satanic *"strong hold"* can withstand the weapons of love, joy, peace, longsuffering, gentleness, goodness, faith, meekness, and self-control. These weapons offer the absolute promise of victory over *"imaginations." "Imaginations"* align my tendency to analyze (over thinking) with a host of emotionally debilitating "what if's" (consuming anxieties).

"Casting down imaginations." A large dose of over analysis coupled with an anxious disposition is an invitation for Satan to gain a "strong hold" in my life. The demonic war against my mind involves subtle thoughts that result in massive amounts of worry and wasted hours of contemplation. This generally happens in the dark silence of my life, somewhere between midnight and sunrise. So persistent is the attack, it refuses to grant me more than a few hours of reprieve through restless sleep. I cling to the hope of *"casting down"* self-induced anxiety-producing analysis (worry).

"Casting down." I can only cast down what I possess. I freely admit my attachment to the anxiety producing analysis of over thinking. Worry has become, in some twisted way, an imaginary blanket of protection against the thing I fear becoming a reality. In other words, "If I worry about it, it won't happen."

"Casting down." I have convinced myself that worry is what caring people do. I have often heard myself say, "I worry about you because I

love you." I have duped myself into believing that worry is the uncon-
querable enemy of my soul. This is more than a delusion, it is a devilish
"strong hold," keeping me hypervigilant, helpless and without hope.

Thought for the Day: I must admit that these thoughts are not always
intrusive; sometimes I willfully welcome them, even invite them.

<u>Search Me, O God!</u>

- Take time to own your ungodly thoughts and to confess them
  to the Lord.

- Analysis + "what if 's" = Imaginations

- How does worrying make you miserable?

- Why do Christians worry?

- How do you respond to the phrase "worry is what caring people
  do"?

- What do you think is the reason we deliberately allow ourselves
  to entertain evil thoughts?

- Does worry make you hypervigilant, helpless and without
  hope?

My "I" Problem with Godly Thinking
"Casting Down Every High Thing"
Day 22

*"Casting down imaginations, and every high
thing that exalteth itself against the knowledge of
God, and bringing into captivity every thought
to the obedience of Christ"*
(2 Corinthians 10:5)

"Casting down." *"Casting down"* (kathaireo) is quite different than the violent *"pulling down"* mentioned in the previous verse. *"Casting down"* implies a nonviolent act of forcefully detaching oneself from unreasonable reasoning ("unreasonable reasoning" is, by far, one of the best definitions of anxious thinking I have ever heard). The spiritual weapons mentioned in the last chapter are the tools I need to conquer paralyzing ruminations that invite Satan's *"strong holds."* Now, that is exactly what I need! My prayer, O Lord, is to receive freedom from over thinking, overreacting, and overanalyzing. I ask that this passage will show the way to victory.

"And every high thing." A *"high thing"* is another way of saying, "a proud thought." I would like to think of myself as humble, but I am all too familiar with the pride that resides in my heart. I know what it is like to live day after day in the emptiness of my own arrogance. These are hard words to say, but I find relief in confessing them. These *"high"* thoughts are the same ones that made Solomon, the world's wisest yet most foolish man, cry out, *"Vanity of vanities, saith the Preacher, vanity of vanities; all is vanity"* (*Ecclesiastes 1:2*). In other words, "Life has no meaning and I feel empty."

"And every high thing." Like Solomon, I have desperately tried to quench my *"high"* thoughts with pleasure, laughter, knowledge, work, materialism, reputation, and multiple indulgences. *"Then,"* in the foot steps of the Ecclesiastical writer, I lament, *"I looked on all the works that my hands had wrought, and on the labour that I had laboured to do: and, behold, all was vanity and vexation of spirit, and there was no profit under the sun"* (*Ecclesiastes 2:11*). The Holy Spirit frequently whispers to my stubborn spirit, "Detach from your prideful self-indulgences." Such whispers of wisdom are easy to hear, but extremely difficult to follow. I am enmeshed with my self-indulgences. Frankly, to disengage from them is undesirable and unthinkable.

"Casting down ... every high thing." It is terribly important not to give place to the Devil. If I do not forcefully detach myself from every proud thought, I quickly become a pawn in the hand of Satan.

Thought for the Day: The Holy Spirit frequently whispers to my stubborn spirit, "Detach from your prideful self-indulgences."

<u>Search Me, O God!</u>

- It is important to detach ourselves from every anxious thought.

- Ask the Holy Spirit to show you what ways are you a proud person.

- What have you attempted to do to quench your prideful thoughts?

- How difficult is self-denial for you?

- Satan is constantly searching for an opening that he can use to attack us.

- How does the Spirit speak to you?

My "I" Problem with Godly Thinking
"Every High Thing"
Day 23

*"Casting down imaginations, and every high
thing that exalteth itself against the knowledge of
God, and bringing into captivity every thought
to the obedience of Christ"
(2 Corinthians 10:5)*

"High thing." Deliberately indulging in unreasonable reasoning (dwelling on anxiety-producing thoughts) is a *"high thing."* Is the Spirit telling me that anxiety is a matter of pride? I hope not, because it seems more like an act of shame and weakness. The words, *"high thing,"* literally refer to an elevated structure used as a barrier in times of war. Anxiety is a barrier effectively separating me from God, which is the last thing I want to happen. When I worry, I feel far from God, because I am casting all my cares upon myself; God is excused from my life and I become my own god.

"High thing." Worry deafens my ears to the Spirit, blinds my eyes to the Word, and depends solely on my reasoning and problem solving skills. Worry dethrones the Father, and insults Son and leaves everything up to me. No wonder anxiety causes me to feel desperate and alone! A thick wall of pride-filled worry keeps me from the heavenly Problem Solver and Comforter of my soul.

"High thing." Fear, left unchecked, transforms itself into something even more debilitating and more destructive: *"the spirit of fear"* (*2 Timothy 1:7*). *"The spirit of fear"* is, in fact, "the Demon of Fear." Now I understand why anxiety-producing analysis is a *"high thing."* Worry is an open invitation for demonic oppression. How foolish I am to welcome into my life *"the spirit of fear"* instead of the three-fold resource *"of power, and of love, and of a sound mind."* Father, at the time, worry seems a reasonable response to my troubles. Increase my trust in your almighty self. Amen.

"Casting down ... every high thing." The violent and unpleasant component in *"casting down"* is the pain I must inflict on myself. Refusing to worry is a painfully difficult chore. I do not find pain, any pain, very appealing. I must keep my eyes on the Problem-Solver rather than the problem at hand. I know that *"God resisteth the proud, and giveth grace to the humble" (1 Peter 5:5)*. Lord, I must confess that my thoughts are not your thoughts. My life is an "I Centered" one. My deceitful heart

quickly rationalizes worry and my ungodly mind readily indulges in it. You are calling me to stop a life-long pattern of worry. I cannot do this on my own. I pray for Holy Spirit enablement to win this battle.

Thought for the Day: A thick wall of pride-filled worry keeps me from the heavenly Problem Solver and Comforter of my soul.

<u>Search Me, O God!</u>

- How is it possible that your anxiety is actually a matter of pride?

- How does worry affect your walk with the Lord?

- How does seeing fear as a demon change your perspective?

- How difficult is it for you not to worry?

- List some practical ways you can focus on the Problem-Solver instead of the problem that you think needs solved.

My "I" Problem with Godly Thinking

"Exalteth Itself . . . Against God

Day 24

*"Casting down imaginations, and every high
thing that exalteth itself against the knowledge of
God, and bringing into captivity every thought
to the obedience of Christ"*
(2 Corinthians 10:5)

"That exalteth itself." I find the wording to be quite interesting. I would have thought it might read, "do not exalt high things above . . . ." Therefore, when I read, *"exalteth itself,"* I am intrigued. How can "high things" exalt themselves? This brings to mind Isaiah's record of the prideful fall of a chief angel by the name of Lucifer. His words are chilling because they reflect the base nature of my own heart apart from God. *"How art thou fallen from heaven, O Lucifer, son of the morning! How art thou cut down to the ground, which didst weaken the nations! For thou hast said in thine heart, I will ascend into heaven, I will exalt my throne above the stars of God: I will sit also upon the mount of the congregation, in the sides of the north: I will ascend above the heights of the clouds; I will be like the most High. Yet thou shalt be brought down to hell, to the sides of the pit." (Isaiah 14:12-15).*

"Exalteth." Satan's five "I will's" reflect the extent of his pride and serve as a powerful warning against my own egotistical potential, especially when the Demon of Fear oppresses my spirit. *"High thing"* is another word for demons. Principalities, powers, rulers of darkness of this world, and spiritual wickedness in high places are a few of the rankings of Hell's demonic powers.

"Against the knowledge of God." The word *"against"* reminds me, once again, of the unseen yet ever-present spiritual warfare Satan wages against my soul. *"Imaginations"* (anxiety producing analysis) and *"every high thing"* (arrogant self-dependency) stand in direct opposition to *"the knowledge of God."* These are Satan's greatest weapons to torture me until I deny my *"knowledge of God"* and indulge in the sin of anxious reflection. Torture is the right word, for it best describes the agony I experience when I deliberately chose to disobey my Lord.

"Against the knowledge of God." I also notice that it doesn't say, "knowledge of God's Word." Rather, it is *"the knowledge of God,"* himself. This is more than knowing principles in God's Word. I must have an intimate, experiential knowledge of the Author of the Book. This

must be what Paul meant when he wrote, *"That I may know him, and the power of his resurrection, and the fellowship of his sufferings, being made conformable unto his death" (Philippians 3:10).* Father, protect me from intellectualizing Christianity to the point that I neglect the relationship my soul longs to have with you.

Thought for the Day: I must have an intimate, experiential knowledge of the Author of the Book.

<u>Search Me, O God!</u>

- What are some common high things that exalt themselves against God?

- It is important to remember that there is a constant battle between "I will" and God's will.

- What is the difference between knowledge about God and knowledge of God?

- There is a constant danger of intellectualizing Christianity.

- May our prayer be that God tears down our walls of pride.

My "I" Problem with Godly Thinking
"Every Thought to the Obedience"
Day 25

*"Casting down imaginations, and every high
thing that exalteth itself against the knowledge of
God, and bringing into captivity every thought
to the obedience of Christ"
(2 Corinthians 10:5)*

"And bringing into captivity every thought." "Every thought," intent, and motive must be captured for God. There is the potential of great harm if I "cast down" anxious ruminations without *"bringing* [them] *into captivity."* This caging keeps me pure and honoring to God. I must never allow my choices, emotions, or attitudes to wander from the holy confinement of the knowledge of God. My thought life must be brought into captivity and kept there; every thought imprisoned by the glorious and holy thoughts of God. Solomon's wisdom must be my passion, *"lean not unto thine own understanding." (Proverbs 3:5b).* I denounce this natural tendency to rely on my insights and calculations, and I resolve to honor him with true, honest, just, pure, and lovely thoughts. Spirit of God, deposit in me the mind of Christ and captivate me with the Words of Life.

"To the obedience of Christ." I need to make certain my everyday life complies with the Word of God. This will not happen until I think the thoughts of God, which is accomplished through *"the renewing of* [my] *mind" (Romans 12:2b).* Obedience is the key: *"Let us hear the conclusion of the whole matter: Fear God, and keep his commandments: for this is the whole duty of man" (Ecclesiastes 12:13.* My obedience is dependent upon my intimacy with God and knowledge of his Word. There is a distinct difference between being obedient to the Word and being obedient to Christ. In the first place, I am obeying rules and regulations. In the second, I am actually obeying the person of God, with whom I have a cherished relationship.

I cannot deny the power and protection *2 Corinthians 10:5* affords me when I refuse my arrogant attempts to analyze the situation and intimately walk in obedience to him. Spiritual conflicts are a highway that I must travel if my destination is spiritual victory. Without exception, all demonic oppression falls at the feet of the Lord of the Word. Moreover, as I live in the conscious presence of Christ, anxiety eventually transforms into unimaginable faith and confidence in Christ. Lord, increase my faith.

Thought for the Day: I denounce this natural tendency to rely on my insights and calculations, and I resolve to honor him with true, honest, just, pure, and lovely thoughts. Spirit of God, deposit in me the mind of Christ.

<u>Search Me, O God!</u>

- What are some thoughts that you must bring into captivity to Christ?

- Living for Christ requires a constant denial of self and focus on Christ.

- It is important to deliberately meditate on God and his Word.

- Do you see a difference between obeying the Word and obeying Christ?

- Spiritual victory is dependent on spiritual conflict. What is your initial reaction to that comment?

- Spend some time denouncing your carnal self and committing to the mind of Christ.

Chapter 6

My "I" Problem
With Being a
Living Sacrifice

Day 26   "I Beseech You Therefore"

Day 27   "Brethren, By the Mercies of God"

Day 28   "Your Bodies, a Living Sacrifice"

Day 29   "Holy, Acceptable unto God"

Day 30   "Your Reasonable Service"

"I beseech you therefore, brethren, by the mercies of God, that ye present your bodies a living sacrifice, holy, acceptable unto God, which is you reasonable service."
(Romans 12:1)

My "I" Problem with Being a Living Sacrifice
"I Beseech You Therefore"
Day 26

"I beseech you therefore, brethren, by the mercies
of God, that ye present your bodies a living sacrifice,
holy, acceptable unto God, which is you reasonable service."
(Romans 12:1)

For as long as I can remember, the word "consecration" has been a part of my Christian vocabulary. It is a term that describes the high level of commitment and devotion a believer has for God. A consecrated life is a fully dedicated life, which is entirely different from a dedicated life. I find it rather easy to dedicate certain parts of my life to the Lord. However, the thought of total release is a less than desirable one. It removes from me the thing I hold most dearly, my self-will. Father, make these *"words of the wise* [be] *as goads, and as nails fastened"* to my heart *(Ecclesiastes 12:11)*.

"I beseech you therefore." The more I think about it, there is something very troubling in these words. There is something very disturbing about an apostle begging me to become *"a living sacrifice."* It is humbling enough to imagine the great apostle Paul imploring me; what's worse, he is only writing what the Spirit directed him to write. Actually, it is not the apostle, but the Holy Spirit who is pleading me to action. I have often stiff-armed God with my willful rebellion. I deserve his wrath, not a gentle word of encouragement. Yet, the Spirit comes along side, nudges, whispers, and urges me to follow the call of consecration. I suppose *"beseech"* is a form of conviction, and I pray for the day when the Spirit will no longer have to convict me to obey. Nevertheless, for now, I thank God for his holy nudges and heavenly conviction.

"Therefore." A curiosity awakens in me and drives me to the preceding chapter in search of answers *(Romans 11)*. "Therefore what," I wonder. It must contain the reason the apostle reduces himself to a beggar, urging me to follow his advice. So, my eyes drift to the last verse of *Romans 11*, which is more than enough to convince me I should heed Paul's forthcoming words. They read, *"For of him, and through him, and to him, are all things: to whom be glory for ever. Amen." (Romans 11:36)*. Everything is *"of"* God, *"through"* God, and *"to"* God. It is not about me; it is about the glory of God. It is high time I give God the control panel of my life, stop self-indulgence pursuits, and establish him as the center around which my life revolves. My disappointments, my

struggles, my opportunities—every bit of everything is about God and God alone.

Thought for the Day: I find it rather easy to dedicate certain parts of my life to the Lord.

<u>Search Me, O God!</u>

- Create a list of things you find difficult to dedicate to the Lord.

- Have you ever experienced Holy Spirit conviction? What is the difference between conviction and guilt?

- Can you recall times when the Spirit convicted you of a particular sin, but no longer does because you have received victory?

- What does Romans 11:36 mean to you?

- How difficult is it to acknowledge that it is not about you, but the glory of God?

- Dedicating your entire self to God is a life-long pursuit.

My "I" Problem with Being a Living Sacrifice
"Brethren, By the Mercies of God"
Day 27

"I beseech you therefore, brethren, by the mercies
of God, that ye present your bodies a living sacrifice,
holy, acceptable unto God, which is you reasonable service."
(Romans 12:1)

"Brethren." The Greek word is "adelphos." It illustrates the bonds of affection among family members. A play on the word "adelphos" reveals its true meaning, "a dear one." "Dear ones" in Christ ought to maintain long-lasting connections with their spiritual family. Many intimate experiences with the family of God readily come to mind. These satisfying and encouraging experiences strengthen my spirit and honor God. However, I cringe at times when family turns against family. Holy Father, this day I commit myself to making positive deposits into the family of God, regardless of denomination, theology, or conviction. May I show these "dear ones" that they are, indeed, dear to me.

"By the mercies of God." Paul goes for the juggler. Not only is he begging; he is appealing to God's *"mercies"* as motivation to obey his next words. I am embarrassed how often I have been unappreciative of God's unmerited *"mercies."* The Psalmist was right when he declared, *"His mercy endureth forever" (Psalms 136).* I might be able to overlook a begging apostle, but I could never ignore my merciful Savior. How could I neglect his gifts of forgiveness, compassion, blessing, provision, and salvation? Lord, ask what you will and, by your Spirit's power, I will do it.

"That ye present your bodies." I have often felt that my body was a hindrance to my spiritual life, *"the spirit indeed is willing, but the flesh is weak" (Matthew 26:41a).* Health problems, mental limitations, emotional weakness, and a smorgasbord of physical pains lead me to consider my body more a hindrance than an asset. How could such an unpleasant obstacle have to potential of being an instrument of God? Yet, I cannot deny the fact that, in large part, my body defines who I am. Even the Lord possessed a body that ate, drank, slept, and felt pain. I now realize that my body is not an obstacle at all, it is the tool through which God chooses to reveal himself to others. My mouth is the Lords; I will speak of him wherever I go. My eyes are his as well; I will look for those who need Jesus. My ears are his ears; I will carefully listen for the Spirit's gentle whispers. I give every bit of my body to my Lord to use as he sees fit.

Thought for the Day: How could I neglect his gifts of forgiveness, compassion, blessing, provision, and salvation? Lord, ask and, by your Spirit's power, I will do it.

Search Me, O God!

- Do you have long-lasting relationships with fellow Christians?

- What can you do to make positive deposits into fellow believers?

- What would it take for you to pray and follow through on the "ask what you will" prayer?

- Often we think that a servant of God becoming ill interrupts God working through them. Why is that?

- What part of your body remains unconsecrated to the Lord?

- How difficult is it to act on what you know is God's will for your life?

My "I" Problem with Being a Living Sacrifice
"Your Bodies a Living Sacrifice"
Day 28

*"I beseech you therefore, brethren, by the mercies
of God, that ye present your bodies a living sacrifice,
holy, acceptable unto God, which is you reasonable service."
(Romans 12:1)*

"That ye present." In the Old Testament, the Levitical priests would *"present"* their sacrifices on the altar before God. The whole process was very elaborate, specific, holy, and bloody. God is calling me to make a conscious, moment-by-moment, dedication of my body to God—placing it on the altar. If he gives me health or sickness, strength or weakness, struggles or serenity, my body is no longer mine; it belongs to God. With all its flaws and imperfections, I *"present"* my body to the one who formed it and breathed into it the breath of life. Lord, here is my body; do with it as you wish. Yet, I must admit, I wonder what good this aging body could be to Almighty God.

"A living sacrifice." Do these words actually belong together? Aren't all sacrifices dead? How can *"living"* and *"sacrifice"* co-exist? Offering my body to God as a *"sacrifice,"* certainly implies death. Dying to self is the ultimate goal of spiritual growth; it is my goal as well. This spiritual death principle is woven throughout the New Testament: *"I am crucified with Christ" (Galatians 2:20a), "baptized into his death" (Romans 6:3b),* and *"planted together in the likeness of his death" (Romans 6:5a).* I must die to my sinful appetites, self-will, and personal opinions. All these, I place on the altar. Help me, O Lord, to keep them in the place of death. I am often tempted to revive them. Sin is enticing and I am weak. The struggle is constant and incredibly intense.

"Living." Dying to self is only one side of the coin. The other side involves life—a *"living sacrifice."* When Paul wrote, *"I am crucified with Christ"* he added, *"nevertheless, I live," (Galatians 2:20).* He explained that though I have been *"baptized into* [Christ's] *death,"* I am to *"walk in newness of life" (Romans 6:4).* When I place my life on the altar, I die to self, and invite the Spirit of God to surge through me with the same spiritual freshness and fervor that possessed Jesus two millennia ago. I have a different life-source that is neither self-centered nor sin-indulgent, for it is the life of Jesus Christ. This must have been what the apostle meant when he wrote, *"Christ in you, the hope of glory" (Colossians*

1:27b). Now I walk, but it is actually his walk; I talk, but the words flow from his lips; and I live, but it is his life to live as he sees fit.

Thought for the Day: Now I walk, but it is actually his walk; I talk, but the words flow from his lips; and I live, yet it is his life to live as he sees fit.

<u>Search Me, O God!</u>

- How does knowing your body actually belongs to God affect you during times of temptation or difficulty?

- Have you offered your body to God for his holy use?

- What does it mean to be a "living sacrifice"?

- What point is Paul making in these three verses?

- What part of your body remains unconsecrated to the Lord?

- If the Spirit of God surges through me with the same spiritual freshness and fervor that possessed Jesus, then (finish the sentence)?

My "I" Problem with Being a Living Sacrifice
"Holy, Acceptable unto God"
Day 29

*"I beseech you therefore, brethren, by the mercies
of God, that ye present your bodies a living sacrifice,
holy, acceptable unto God, which is you reasonable service."
(Romans 12:1)*

"Present your bodies a living sacrifice." At first glance, presenting my body to God appears to be the first of three things the apostle commands in this verse. If so, the other two expectations are becoming *"holy"* and being *"acceptable unto God."* Actually, holiness and being acceptable before God are the results of offering my body as God's living sacrifice. This requires that I make a very determined and deeply spiritual, presentation of myself before him, offering my body to be *"a living sacrifice."* Lord, many times I have toyed with the idea of the consecrated life, made a half-hearted offer of myself to you, but have never truly followed through. Today, I give myself to you. No longer is it my life, it is yours to do with as you wish. I will not dictate the direction I am to go, nor will I question the choices you make. On those occasions when I fail, and I know I will, I will immediately confess, remember this once and for all presentation, and readily renew my vow to be your *"living sacrifice."*

"Holy, acceptable unto God." Exchanging my life for Christ's life is the only way to holiness and acceptance before God. My pursuit of living a *"holy"* life is useless unless I walk in Christ's holiness. The same is true of being *"acceptable."* There is nothing *"acceptable"* about me (*Romans 3:10*). If God is pleased with me, it will be Christ's doing and not my own. *"And be found in him, not having mine own righteousness, which is of the law, but that which is through the faith of Christ, the righteousness which is of God by faith" (Philippians 3:9).*

"Holy." The Greek word translated *"holy"* actually does not mean purity, as I have often heard. "Hagios" simply means, "to set one's self apart for God." Yielding my life to God sets me apart for one purpose—God's purpose. Whereas before I was set apart for my own interests, I now have a higher reason to exist. My life is for him and no other. Of course, now that I am set apart for his use, it is imperative that I remain uncontaminated by sin. Being set apart for God means that, not only am I made pure and holy by him, but that I remain pure and holy for him.

Thought for the Day: This requires that I make a very determined and deeply spiritual, presentation of myself before him, offering my body to be *"a living sacrifice."*

<u>Search Me, O God!</u>

- When you accept Christ as Savior, you receive God's forgiveness and salvation.

- When you present your body a living sacrifice, you receive God's holiness and acceptance.

- Why do Christians toy with the idea of living the consecrated life, but seldom follow through?

- After reading Galatians 2:20, how would you describe what has been called "the exchanged life"?

- What is implied in the notion that we are set apart for God's use?

- Who do you know that lives such a life?

- What keeps you from doing this?

My "I" Problem with Being a Living Sacrifice
"Your Reasonable Service"
Day 30

"I beseech you therefore, brethren, by the mercies
of God, that ye present your bodies a living sacrifice,
holy, acceptable unto God, which is you reasonable service."
(Romans 12:1)

"Which is your reasonable service." The "I for Christ" exchange is not only logical and sensible; it is highly worshipful. This holy transformation is quite possibly the highest act of worship I can offer God this side of Heaven. I have a God-given *"service,"* to exchange my life for his, to offer him glory and honor, and to remain *"fit for the Master's use, prepared unto every good work."*

"Reasonable Service." It is simple logic. Since Jesus Christ has saved my soul, forgiven my sins, and promised me eternity, and since the Holy Spirit resides in me, convicts me, and guides me into all truth, and since the Father has blessed me with all spiritual blessings, made me accepted in the beloved, and calls me his son, it simply makes good sense that I offer my life to God.

"Service." Often, we say that pastors, missionaries, Christian school teachers, and so on are "in the ministry," or "in fulltime Christian service." Those phrases are terribly misleading. Every person that claims Christ as Savior is "in fulltime Christian service." I must avoid categorizing Christianity and start viewing it as a life-long call to consecration and service of Jesus Christ.

I can hardly wait to digest the next verse. *"And be not conformed to this world; but be ye transformed by the renewing of your mind, that ye may prove what is that good, and acceptable, and perfect, will of God"* (*Romans 12:2* But, for now, I celebrate that my body belongs to God and is the *"temple of the Holy Ghost"* (*1 Corinthians 6:19*).

I will *"glorify God in* [my] *body, and in* [my] *spirit, which are God's"* (*1 Corinthians 6:20*). This is the consecrated life my spirit longs for and the consecrated life I will pursue. Lord, more than anything else, I want to be used by you. I want to be your servant. I long for you to live your life through me. Help me to remain conscious that I am in your service and for your glory. Being *"a living sacrifice"* is a *"reasonable service"* after all you have done for me.

Thought for the Day: The "I for Christ" exchange is not only logical and sensible; it is highly worshipful. This holy transformation is quite possibly the highest act of worship I can offer God this side of Heaven.

<u>Search Me, O God!</u>

- How could the exchanged life be the height of worship?

- Is it unreasonable for God to expect you to deny yourself, take up your cross, and follow him?

- How would your life change if you live as though you were in fulltime Christian service?

- Romans 12:1,2 are essential to our spiritual development.

- Does your spirit long for a deeper walk with the Lord?

- How can giving God your body be an ongoing worship experience?

Chapter 7

My "I" Problem
With Renewing
My Mind

Day 31   "And Be Not . . . But Be Ye"

Day 32   "Be Not Conformed to this World"

Day 33   "But Be Ye Transformed"

Day 34   "Renewing of Your Mind"

Day 35   "Good, and Acceptable, and Perfect"

"And be not conformed to this world; but be ye transformed by the renewing of your mind, that ye may prove what is that good, and acceptable, and perfect will of God."
(Romans 12:2)

My "I" Problem with Renewing My Mind
"And Be Not . . . But Be Ye"
Day 31

"And be not conformed to this world; but be ye transformed by the renewing of your mind, that ye may prove what is that good, and acceptable, and perfect will of God."
(Romans 12:2)

I cannot think of a greater challenge than changing the way I think. So, I am not at all encouraged by the theme of renewing my mind, which ranks somewhere between very hard and nigh to impossible. But, this is God's Word and I am his child. I hesitantly enter this study admitting weakness and trusting that God will accomplish what I cannot for myself.

"And be not . . . but be ye." At first glance, these phrases oppose my natural way of <u>doing</u> things. I am a doer and would prefer to read, "Do not," and "do." I have often been deceived by today's conduct-oriented society that limits Christianity to an exhausting list of unattainable do's and don'ts. From a child, I have learned to do the appropriate and shun the inappropriate. On many occasions, I have stifled the mystical side of faith by over-emphasizing morals and values. Faith in Christ involves much more than rules and regulations. These *"be"* words are mind and character words and far more accurately measures my spiritual maturity than compliance to a set of laws (which was the Old Testament way). Standing alone, conduct is dreadfully inferior, and horribly superficial. In one word, conduct without character is simply hypocritical. I must be careful that what I do for the Lord is soul-based rather than performance-based. So, I wonder, what the Holy Spirit is calling me to *"be"* and not to *"be."*

"And be not . . . but be ye." Paul's emphasizes character over conduct, a dynamic change from inside out. One of the evils in today's version of Christianity is appearance over substance. Though *"man looketh on the outward appearance, ... the Lord looketh on the heart"* (*1 Samuel 16:7b*). Satan, the expert deceiver finds it rather easy to imitate Christianity with *"outward appearance*[s]*."* At times, I have wrongly assumed that Satan is intent on attacking my doing. Rather, he goes for the heart, my character. When God changes my heart, my feet follow. Yet, when I change my feet (behaviors), my heart (attitudes) may still be far from him. Though I live by Christian virtues, if God has not initiated a change of heart, I deceive others as Satan has deceived me. Yet, God looks beyond my religious facade and knows the condition of my heart (the warning of *Matthew 7:21-23* is inescapable).

Thought for the Day: These *"be"* words are mind and character words and far more accurately measures my spiritual maturity than compliance to a set of laws.

Search Me, O God!

- How difficult is it for you to change your way of thinking, or you attitude?

- Do you believe that many have reduced Christianity to mere behaviors?

- Does character come from conduct or conduct from character?

- Is it easier for Satan to counterfeit conduct or character?

- How could someone declare that Jesus is "Lord, Lord" only to hear he proclaim, "And then will I profess unto them, I never knew you: depart from me, ye that work iniquity." (Matthew 7:21-23)

- How would your life change with this as your life's mission?

My "I" Problem with Renewing My Mind
"Be Not Conformed to this World"
Day 32

"And be not conformed to this world; but be ye transformed by the renewing of your mind, that ye may prove what is that good, and acceptable, and perfect will of God."
(Romans 12:2)

"Be not conformed." Conformity reminds me of those who hold on to conventional and traditional ways. Once upon a time, I was all about change. Change meant progress, accomplishment, and discovery. However, as I mature (okay, age) I have settled into some very predictable patterns. I know all too well the meaning of the axiom, "Old habits are hard to break." *"Conform"* is a fashion word, calling us to keep up with current trends and so-called advances. Today's spiritual trend appears to reduce God to a series of meaningless and useless rituals, making followers of Christ inferior replicas of those who adhered to the old time religion. Conformity is all too easy, but thoughts of a spiritual revolution are invigorating.

"Be not conformed to the world." I am surprised that *"world"* is "aion" and not the Greek word "cosmos." If it were "cosmos," the call would be to avoid the sinful contaminations of this fallen world, sinful habits that characterize the ungodly. However, the Spirit of God carefully chose the tiny, but powerful word "aion," which warns me against my natural, logical, and common sense self. Just because it makes good sense, or seems reasonable is not a godly enough reason to do it. Conforming to the natural way of things is an insult to the supernatural ways of God. It makes me a practical atheist (living without consulting God is the same as living without God) and demotes me to the finite wisdom of fallen humanity. Lord, give me a heart for the supernatural, a mind for the holy, and a hunger for righteousness. May I shun the world's ever-enticing logic.

"But." This common and simple word keeps me in line and convicts me when I go *"out of the way."* It highlights the sharp contrast between God's ways and the ways of the world. However tiny and seemingly insignificant, *"but"* has kept me from many acts of disobedience. One of the Holy Spirit's greatest tasks must be to interrupt my worldly plans and behaviors with the power-filled "buts'" of Scripture. When I try to flee from God's presence, the Spirit greets me with a soul wrenching *"But the Lord" (Jonah 1:4).* When I face insurmountable obstacles, he

whispers to my heart, *"But God" (Ephesians 2:4).* "Alla," translated *"but,"* injects a razor-sharp objection into my worldly tendencies.

Thought for the Day: Conforming to the natural way of things is an insult to the supernatural ways of God.

<u>Search Me, O God!</u>

- What is the value or danger of "old shoe" Christianity?

- Do you believe the average professing believer is an inferior replica of Christ?

- Just because it makes good sense, or seems reasonable is not a godly enough reason to do it. Is it easier for Satan to counterfeit conduct or character?

- Do you have a heart for the supernatural?

- How do you relate to the power-filled "buts" of Scripture?

- What do you think about this statement?

My "I" Problem with Renewing My Mind
"But Be Ye Transformed"
Day 33

"And be not conformed to this world; but be ye transformed by the renewing of your mind, that ye may prove what is that good, and acceptable, and perfect will of God."
(Romans 12:2)

"Be ye transformed." These words haunt my spirit and exhaust my soul. They force me to go against my natural cravings to conform to worldly ways. Paul would have pronounced it "met-am-or-fo'-o," which sounds a lot like metamorphosis (a supernatural change from one form into another). Anything supernatural requires more than I could ever produce, introducing God's presence and power into the matter. Suddenly, its haunting gives way to hope, the hope of the divine intervention of the Holy Spirit enabling me to accomplish what would otherwise be impossible. Lord, I open my heart to your transforming power. Mold me and shape me as your wish.

"Transformed." This type of supernatural revolution is a life-long journey involving periods of rapid growth, times of apparent stagnation, trials that bring me to my knees, and intense struggles with sin. Rapid growth is the exhilarating part of these experiences. Stagnation often leaves me feeling dissatisfied with God or disregarded by him. And, of course, bringing me to my knees and intense struggles with sin are extremely discouraging. Generally, each step in my spiritual journey has been interrupted with brief reprieve before the process resumes. The goal of transformation is both destructive and constructive—breaking me of myself and drawing me closer to my God. The path to transformation is called the *"renewing of* [my] *mind."*

"Your mind." Do we really need to go here? My *"mind"* is the only thing completely, or at least mostly, concealed from others. *Ezekiel* called it *"the chambers of imagery" (8:12)*. My *"mind"* is the place of contemplation where motives are created and purposes are established. This is my private world and no one has entrance into it without my approval. In my *"mind,"* I reason, feel, judge, fantasize, idealize, and justify. Experience, heredity, and personality solidify my opinions, prejudices, desires, and cravings. If God is speaking of transforming my *"mind,"* I am facing a most difficult journey. This old *"mind"* is set in its ways and doesn't take kindly an invitation to develop new habits or thoughts.

Thought for the Day: Anything supernatural requires more than I could ever produce, introducing God's presence and power into the matter. The path to transformation is called the *"renewing of* [my] *mind."*

Search Me, O God!

- Has the Holy Spirit ever intervened on your behalf?

- Think about your lifelong journey. Did it involve growth, stagnation, trials, and temptation?

   - Growth

   - Stagnation

   - Trials

   - Temptation

- If people could read my mind, (finish the sentence)!

- Proof of the supernatural is in God doing for you what you can't without him.

My "I" Problem with Renewing My Mind
"Renewing of Your Mind"
Day 34

"And be not conformed to this world; but be ye transformed by the renewing of your mind, that ye may prove what is that good, and acceptable, and perfect will of God."
(Romans 12:2)

"By the renewing of your mind." Holy renewal involves a total make-over. I must first be broken down before a holy renovation can begin. This is beginning to make sense. The Holy Spirit is not interested in making me a better man; he wants to remake me altogether. If I attempt to blend God's ways with my preconceived notions and biased biases, I will, at best, become a more moral and compassionate person. However, that is not the Spirit's ambition for my life.

"By the renewing of your mind." His transformation demands an emptying of my style of thinking, reasoning, ethics, religion, morals, and so much more. It is only after being emptied that he makes a holy deposit in my spirit. So, what is that holy deposit? It is the mind of God. This divine transaction causes his will to become my will, his pleasure is suddenly my pleasure, his wisdom is my wisdom, and his passion is my passion. In the end, there is a divine metamorphosis of my capacity for love, forgiveness, mercy, joy, peace, patience, perseverance, acceptance, and much more. In truth, this is the path to Paul's ultimate passion: *"Yet not I, but Christ" (Galatians 2:20)*. Paul's ultimate passion is quickly becoming mine.

"That ye may prove." God's divine transformation of my soul equips me to scrutinize every experience, every thought, every word, every opportunity, and every relationship. In the end, I discover *"what is that good, and acceptable, and perfect will of God."* I long to know his divine providence for my life, receive his nod of approval, and experience the fullness of God.

"Will of God." With a renewed mind, I receive spiritual clarity. With a renewed mind, I set my affections on the *"will of God."* With a renewed mind, I yearn to do only what pleases him. Honoring God is the natural outcome of having my mind renewed. *"For it is God who worketh in you both to will and to do of his good pleasure" (Philippians 2:13)*. Lord, create in me a new heart that beats for you, seeks your will, and honors you above all else.

Thought for the Day: It is the mind of God. This divine transaction causes his will to become my will, his pleasure is suddenly my pleasure, his wisdom is my wisdom, and his passion is my passion.

Search Me, O God!

- What is the Spirit's ambition for your life?

- Why must we be emptied before the Spirit makes his deposits in us?

- Everything must be put to the test, whether it is or is not honoring to God.

- In what area of your life do you need your mind renewed?

- This is not something that comes naturally and is evidence of spiritual maturity.

My "I" Problem with Renewing My Mind
"Good, Acceptable, and Perfect"
Day 35

"And be not conformed to this world; but be ye transformed by the renewing of your mind, that ye may prove what is that good, and acceptable, and perfect will of God."
(Romans 12:2)

"Good ... Will of God." God's will for my life is *"good."* In other words, God's will gives my life meaning, value, and purpose. It enables me to make an eternal impact through *"good works"* (things I do for God in the power of his Holy Spirit). Influencing others for God gives my life supreme significance, makes me a man of destiny, and offers God the worship he deserves. Knowing the *"good ... will of God"* actually the word is better translated "excellent," means that I can expect God's very best for my life.

"Acceptable ... Will of God." Knowing and living God's will is the one and only way to please him. Without spiritual consecration, I would surely do what pleases my natural, carnal desires. God's mind renewing transformation makes it possible to deny myself and please him. Otherwise, life would be a pursuit of self-indulgence and self-satisfaction. When I choose God's pleasure over my pleasure, I am definitely walking in his will.

"Prefect ... Will of God." *"Perfect"* means complete, full, and ultimate. Seeking God's will for employment, finances, relationships, and other seemingly important decisions in life is good, but shortsighted. The higher level of God's will, making all other pursuits inferior, is the consecrated life— *"the renewing of* [my] *mind."* It is the will of my Father that I release control of my life and place it into his almighty hands. Lord, this will not come naturally. But, I devote myself to follow your heart's desires.

Lord, I leave this verse with conviction, confession, and commitment. My promise is to daily meditate on your Word, knowing that it will renew my distorted worldly way of thinking.

"I beseech you therefore, brethren, by the mercies of God, that ye present your bodies a living sacrifice, holy, acceptable unto God, which is your reasonable service" (Romans 12:1)

And be not conformed to this world: but be ye transformed by the renewing of your mind, that ye may prove what is that good, and acceptable, and perfect, will of God" (Romans 12:2)

Thought for the Day: Influencing others for God gives my life supreme significance, makes me a man of destiny, and offers God the worship he deserves.

<u>Search Me, O God!</u>

- Influencing others for God gives my life supreme significance, makes me a man of destiny, and offers God the worship he deserves.

- Without Holy Spirit intervention, we would never be able to deny ourselves.

- Seeking God's will in practical matters without striving for the consecrated life is presumptuous.

- We must daily rescue our minds from distorted worldly thinking.

- This is the finish line in our search for significance.

Chapter 8

My "I" Problem
With My Faith
Being Tested

Day 36   "Ye Greatly Rejoice"

Day 37   "A Season [of] Temptations"

Day 38   "If Need Be . . . In Heaviness"

Day 39   "Your Faith . . . Though it be Tried"

Day 40   "Praise and Honour and Glory"

*"Wherein ye greatly rejoice, though now, for a season,
if need be, ye are in heaviness through manifold
temptations: That the trial of your faith, being much more
precious than of gold that perisheth, though it be tried
with fire, might be found unto praise and honour and
glory at the appearing of Jesus Christ."*
(1 Peter 1:6)

My "I" Problem with My Faith Being Tested
"Ye Greatly Rejoice"
Day 36

*"Wherein ye greatly rejoice, though now, for a season, if need be, ye
are in heaviness through manifold temptations: That the trial of your
faith, being much more precious than of gold that perisheth, though
it be tried with fire,
might be found unto praise and honour and glory
at the appearing of Jesus Christ."*
(1 Peter 1:6)

*A*s superficial as it may sound, I just want to be happy. Is that such a bad
thing to ask of God? Some Christians leave me thinking that happiness
is unattainable, and the pursuit of it is quite worldly. Others give the
impression God's greatest desire is that his children be happy, even if it
means they have to compromise biblical standards to get it. Yet, happiness is one of the inescapable themes of Scripture. *1 Peter 1:6, 7* strongly
suggests that God wants me to *"greatly rejoice."* Now, what that means
is yet to be seen, but it is quite apparent that God is highly interested in
me being very happy.

"Wherein ye greatly rejoice." Happiness is not the issue; my source of
happiness is. *"Wherein"* briefly distracts my attention from these verses
and places it on the preceding ones. What I discover is the foundation
of Christian happiness. The first cause for rejoicing is the salvation of
my soul by the resurrection of Jesus Christ from the dead (*verse 3*).
Sadly, there are times when I exchange the joy of my salvation for a
moment or two of fading happiness. Secondly, the promise of eternity in
Heaven should ignite great joy in me, unless I over-estimate the importance of the here-and-now (*verse 4*). Shouldn't the prospects of eternity outweigh whatever happens in the here-and-now? Finally, God's
interest and intervention in my daily circumstances is reason enough to
rejoice (*verse 5*). Lord, I *"rejoice"* that you are my constant companion
through life. The only sustaining happiness available to me on this side
of Heaven comes from three divine gifts: salvation, Heaven, and divine
intervention. Lord, when I lose my happiness, help me to reflect on
the joy of my salvation, the promise of eternity in Heaven, and your
constant watch-care over my life.

"Rejoice." Admittedly, my fleshly self finds little consolation in *verses
3-5*. My search for happiness is more along the lines of an *Ecclesiastes
3* experience—trying everything and gaining nothing. Until I accept the

painful reality that nothing on earth can satisfy my happy-hungry soul, my search will never turn upward. Looking upward brings me to the footstool of the Heavenly Father, his wonderful mercies, and eternal promises.

Thought for the Day: Happiness is one of the inescapable themes of Scripture. However, happiness is not the issue; my source of happiness is. Lord, I *"rejoice"* that you are my constant companion through life.

Search Me, O God!

- Do you think happiness and faith are compatible?

- Happiness is not the issue; my source of happiness is?

- Take time to rejoice that Jesus has saved your soul.

- Take time to rejoice that Heaven is your home.

- Take time to rejoice that God is interested in you.

- How disappointed are you that earth cannot satisfy your hunger for happiness?

- What is (not should be) your source of happiness?

My "I" Problem with My Faith Being Tested
"A Season [of] Temptation"
Day 37

"Wherein ye greatly rejoice, though now, for a season, if need be, ye are in heaviness through manifold temptations: That the trial of your faith, being much more precious than of gold that perisheth, though it be tried with fire,
might be found unto praise and honour and glory
at the appearing of Jesus Christ."
(1 Peter 1:6)

"Ye greatly rejoice." How am I supposed to *"greatly rejoice"*? Those who are naturally less expressive tell me that this is an inward experience of peace and contentment. They suggest that it is vital to remain in silent awe before the King of kings and the Lord of lords. Those who are more expressive seem convinced that the experience includes shouting, jumping, and a wide assortment of behaviors. Heaven, they tell us, is a hot bed of loud expressions of worship. Nevertheless, I wonder, should my natural personality type dictate my spiritual expressions? Aren't there times when it is best to express the joy of the Lord with a single tear, in complete silence—unspoken intimacy with God? And, isn't it equally true that there are times when the joy of the Lord spontaneously explodes with shouting, singing, clapping, and even laughter? Hushed wonder and thunderous celebration are my unfailing companions during times of trials and temptations.

"Though now." It is amazing how two simple words can so quickly change my emotions. My spirit sighs when I read them. *"Though now"* seems to imply that life will offer a strong challenge to my prospects of happiness. *"Now"* is not always a pleasant place to be. At times, it is a place of family stress, time restraints, work demands, and health concerns. Yet, when all is going well, *"now"* remains a foreign country for a soul created to be in the presence of God, a constant struggle against the kingdom of Hell, and a deep yearning to be *"absent from the body, and present with the Lord."*

"Manifold temptations." When I see the word *"temptations,"* I tend to think of the lure and lust of sin. However, the word actually has little to do with sin. Rather, it speaks of trials, which are far more encompassing than the lure of sin. Trials are God ordained appointments I have with troubles and obstacles—each unique and unpredictable. Quite honestly, the promise of *"manifold"* trials is not very encouraging news. I can

endure and even expect occasional trials, but *"manifold"* trials exhaust me. They are challenging, constant, and chronic. Why would God allow his children to suffer such abuse? Surely, there must be a reason.

Thought for the Day: Hushed wonder and thunderous celebration are my unfailing companions during times of trials and temptations.

Search Me, O God!

- How would you describe your worship style? How biblical is it?

- Should our natural personality types dictate our worship of God?

- The deepest trials and the highest joys leave us longing for something more, which only Heaven can fully satisfy.

- What do you think of the statement "trials are God ordained appointments I have with troubles and obstacles"?

- Does your worship of God include both of these?

My "I" Problem with My Faith Being Tested
"If Need Be . . . In Heaviness"
Day 38

"Wherein ye greatly rejoice, though now, for a season, if need be, ye are in heaviness through manifold temptations: That the trial of your faith, being much more precious than of gold that perisheth, though it be tried with fire, might be found unto praise and honour and glory at the appearing of Jesus Christ."
(1 Peter 1:6)

"For a season." This reminds me that the intense and multiple trials of life, which often rob me of joy and threaten my faith, are limited to *"a season."* Seasons of trials are inevitable, inescapable and eventually pass. Thank God, there is a limit to my *"season"* of trials.

"If need be." As difficult as it is to admit, there are times when I *"need"* hardship, chastening, and *"manifold trials."* A string of uneventful days poses an unseen but real threat to my walk with God, making me lazy, careless, and self-confident. Of course, what I call *"need"* and what God calls *"need"* are two different things. A new set of trials appear and I cry out, "I don't need this!" Yet, my God exclaims, "Yes you do."

"Ye are in heaviness." The Christian life is not for the weak of heart. Those who claim that a believer should never be depressed ought to spend more time meditating on these words. *"Heaviness"* is a deeply emotional and all-consuming sense of sorrow, grief, and depression. I am thankful that my Lord understands how challenging and emotionally exhausting the trials of life are. In one brief verse, Peter has taken me from happiness to *"heaviness."* I think he is saying that the way to true happiness is through the deep waters of *"heaviness."*

"Ye greatly rejoice ... ye are in heaviness." Rejoicing during times of intense sorrow is a hallmark of Christianity. Often my tears are not tears of doubt, but a mystical blend of grief and faith. Therefore, I know I can cry and still keep the faith.

"That the trial of your faith." The word, *"that,"* introduces the reason God allows me to experience *"manifold temptations."* However, before he offers the reason, he makes certain I understand that my *"faith"* is on *"trial."* I do not naturally think in these terms. I speak of the trial of finances, the trial of conflicts, the trial of health, or the trial of obstacles, but Scripture refers to such things as *"the trial of* [my] *faith."* Every

trial, from minor irritants to life threatening, is a trial of faith. How will my faith in God respond to a financial need? How will my faith sustain me through conflicts, illnesses, and a host of difficulties? In the flesh, I am more inclined to pray for solutions than for my faith to increase.

Thought for the Day: I am thankful that my Lord understands how exhausting the trials of life are. The way to true happiness is through the deep waters of *"heaviness."*

Search Me, O God!

- How encouraging is it that trials are for a "season"?

- Do you believe that "a string of uneventful days poses an unseen but real threat to [our] walk with God"?

- What do you think about a depressed believer?

- How does you life line up with the "hallmark"?

- Our faith is on trial every moment of our lives.

- Happiness through "heaviness" is one of the paradoxes of the Christian life.

My "I" Problem with My Faith Being Tested
"You Faith . . . Through It Be Tried"
Day 39

"Wherein ye greatly rejoice, though now, for a season, if need be, ye are in heaviness through manifold temptations: That the trial of your faith, being much more precious than of gold that perisheth, though it be tried with fire, might be found unto praise and honour and glory at the appearing of Jesus Christ."
(1 Peter 1:6)

"Being much more precious." From God's perspective, my many faith-trials are not simply *"precious,"* or *"more precious,"* they are *"much more precious."* Now, this is a rather shocking perspective. How can the pains, trials, and struggles of life, for which I have an overdeveloped need to seek deliverance, be *"much more precious"*? Although my spirit peaks with curiosity, my flesh is beginning to feel annoyed with God's promise of more and more trials.

"Than of gold that perisheth." Struggles, stresses, and sufferings are not only needful; they are invaluable. *"Gold"* is a worthless stone in the face of faith-trials. I have lived my life thinking that deliverance from faith-trials is *"much more precious than of gold that perisheth."* I have often pleaded with God, asking him to flex his omnipotent muscles and deliver me from the very thing he calls *"much more precious than of gold that perisheth."* Father, help me to gain and maintain the heavenly perspective that faith-trials are of immeasurable worth. Help me to understand and appreciate its worth, as revealed in the closing words of *verse 7.*

"Though it be tried with fire." All impurities are removed when gold is *"tried in the fire" (Revelation 3:18).* It is the only way to purify gold and the only way to increase its value. The same principle applies to my life. I shouldn't be surprised if my faith-trials seem as intense as the refiner's fire. It is the only way sin can be extinguished and I become useful to God. When tossed in the fiery furnace of faith-trials, I must bear in mind it is precious for my holiness and usefulness to God.

"Might be found unto praise." What *"might be found unto praise"*? The answer is "[my] *faith."* The particular word appears only eleven times in the New Testament. It means words of commendation, approval, or praise. Imagine God commending me for my faithfulness to him during the difficult trials of life. Imagine God commending me for my increased

faith in him because of those same trials. I can think of no higher ambition than to hear the Father declare, *"Well done."*

Thought for the Day: I have often pleaded with God, asking him to flex his omnipotent muscles and deliver me from the very thing he calls *"much more precious than of gold that perisheth."*

<u>Search Me, O God!</u>

- How can the pains, trials, and struggles of life be "much more precious"?

- This concept may be more easily understood than it is to live.

- How can faith-trials be precious for my holiness and usefulness to God?

- Take a few moments and envision the scene.

- Our prayer lives often resist God's will.

My "I" Problem with My Faith Being Tested
"Praise, Honour, and Glory"
Day 40

"Wherein ye greatly rejoice, though now, for a season, if need be, ye are in heaviness through manifold temptations: That the trial of your faith, being much more precious than of gold that perisheth, though it be tried with fire,
might be found unto praise and honour and glory
at the appearing of Jesus Christ."
(1 Peter 1:6)

"Might be found unto praise." The trial will eventually pass, but God's words of commendation will ring in my ears throughout eternity. This is the first eternal consequence of remaining faithful through faith-trials.

"Might be found unto ... honour." The second eternal consequence is *"honour."* *"Praise"* comes through words, while *"honour"* comes through actions. Jesus put it this way in the Sermon on the Mount, *"great is your reward in Heaven" (Matthew 5:12).* The trial of fire will eventually end, but rewards will last throughout eternity. Whether it is the honor of privilege, position, or possessions, my struggles on earth do not go unnoticed by Heaven. Father, help me to remember that everything in my life is packed full of eternal consequences.

"Might be found unto ... glory." At first, the final eternal consequence of enduring faith-trials in Peter's list is a bit confusing. What is the promised *"glory"* after trials have passed? Paul put it this way, *"If so be that we suffer with him, that we may be also glorified together" (Romans 8:17b).* Whereas *"praise"* comes through words and *"honour"* through actions, *"glorified"* is the condition of the soul. A glorified soul is set free from sin and death and exists in a glorified body! My spirit is exhilarated by the prospects of being freed from death and sin.

"Might be found unto praise and honour and glory." If this is the condition of my soul, it is certainly not because I am worthy. If I am to ever maneuver successfully through faith-trials it will ultimately be God's doing and not my own. Holy Spirit, do for me what I am unable to do for myself.

"At the appearing of Jesus Christ." My happiness must not be dependent upon a problem free life or the need to be rescued from every trial. Today's happiness is actually an anticipated happiness, anticipation of *"the appearing of Jesus Christ."*

Lord, while I live in the present, keep me mindful of my future. I long for the day when I shall see you in all your glory. May the anticipation of that day be my source of happiness in trials.

Thought for the Day: Today's happiness is an anticipated happiness, anticipation of *"the appearing of Jesus Christ."*

<u>Search Me, O God!</u>

- Keep your eyes on the finish line!

- Heaven is keenly aware of the struggles we have on eaerth.

- You and I were made for glory. Nothing else will satisfy.

- Never trust in your own strength. Always be God-dependent.

- What does it take to be happy? Anticipation of "the appearing of Jesus Christ."

- Allow this principle to be etched on your soul.

Chapter 9

My "I" Problem
With Not Loving
The World

Day 41   "Love Not"

Day 42   "Love Not the World"

Day 43   "If any Man Love the World"

Day 44   "All That Is in the World"

Day 45   "Is Not of the Father"

"Love not the world, neither the things that are in the world. If any man love the world, the love of the Father is not in him. For all that is in the world, the lust of the flesh, the lust of the eyes, and the pride of life, is not of the Father, but is of the world."
(1 John 2:15-16)

My "I" Problem with Not Loving the World
"Love Not"
Day 41

*"Love not the world, neither the things that are in the world. If any
man love the world, the love of the Father is not in him. For all that
is in the world, the lust of the flesh, the lust
of the eyes, and the pride of life, is not of the Father,
but is of the world."
(1 John 2:15-16)*

Some of Jesus' final words were, *"If ye were of the world, the world
would love his own: but because ye are not of the world, but I have chosen
you out of the world, therefore the world hateth you" (John 15:19).* It is
no surprise that the world is my enemy, but it is very surprising how
attached I have become to this ever-present adversary. I pray that the
Spirit will guide me from infatuation with the world into his glorious
love. Holy Spirit, pour truth into my innermost being and make me more
like the Master.

"Love." I suppose that, as long as I live in this body of flesh, I will
struggle to attain and maintain the ultimate expression of Christian
"love," pronounced "agapao" in the Greek New Testament. In a moment
of unedited authenticity, I realize that I naturally limit my affection to
those who *"love"* me. Jesus strongly condemned such love-limits when
he declared, *"Love your enemies, bless them that curse you, do good to
them that hate you ... that ye may be the children of your Father which is
in heaven" (Matthew 5:44,45).* This is supernatural *"love"* and, as such,
requires divine enablement. Father, I realize apart from divine intervention, I am unable to *"love"* unconditionally. Take me beyond myself, fill
me with your *"love,"* and cause me to *"love"* without limits.

"Love." My affection must go in three very specific directions (see
Deuteronomy 6:5; Matthew 22:37-40). First, I must have heart, soul,
strength, and mind *"love"* for God. This, of course, is the first and
greatest commandment. Secondly, I am to *"love"* my *"neighbor"* to the
same degree as I *"love"* myself. Lastly, I am to *"love"* myself. *"Love"*
is primarily, if not entirely, people focused. Yet, for the most part, people
are difficult to love, myself included.

"Love not." While called to *"love"* without limits, I cannot forget there
are things not fit for me to *"love."* To *"love"* is divine; to *"love not"*
is divine as well. *"Love"* is an attachment that makes me vulnerable,

devoted, and tolerant. Such an attachment demands two inflexible limits: *"love not the world"* and *"neither the things that are in the world."*

Thought for the Day: First, I must have heart, soul, strength, and mind *"love"* for God. Secondly, I am to *"love"* my *"neighbor"* to the same degree as I *"love"* myself. Lastly, I am to *"love"* myself.*"*

<u>Search Me, O God!</u>

- What is there about the world that makes it so enticing to those who seek after God?

- Think of those you truly love. Do you set love-limits (limiting your affection to those who love you back)?

- Do you find one of the three directions of love more difficult than the other two?

- What do you think about the statement "love not is divine as well"?

- What are the implications of loving your neighbor "as yourself"?

My "I" Problem with Not Loving the World
"Love Not the World"
Day 42

"Love not the world, neither the things that are in the world. If any man love the world, the love of the Father is not in him. For all that is in the world, the lust of the flesh, the lust of the eyes, and the pride of life, is not of the Father, but is of the world."
(1 John 2:15-16)

"Love not." The ability to *"love"* and *"love not"* are the divine enablements of the Holy Spirit. Since *"love"* is an attachment, I must know what to *"love"* and not to *"love."* *"Love"* has two inflexible boundaries: *"love not the world"* and *"neither the things that are in the world."*

"Love not the world." This is boundary number one. The *"world,"* known as "cosmos," is undeserving of my affection. The "cosmos" is everything that sets itself against God, draws me away from God, or simply excludes God. "Cosmos" is more than the things I experience with my senses; it is a direct reference to the relentless attacks of a fallen *"world"* on my relationship with God. In other words, "do not form an attachment to this present evil age." My deceitful and desperately wicked heart naturally lives in the present, often forgetting that I am not a citizen of this *"world."* As a citizen of Heaven, I will *"set [my] affection on things above, not on things on the earth" (Colossians 3:2).* A moment of indulgence can easily lead to a life-long attachment. The risk is too great; I must choose to *"love not the world."*

"Love not." *"Love not"* is a negative, it tells me what not to do. So, what should I do with the world's constant bombardment against my walk with God? I am to avoid it, walk away from it, remove it, despise it, and even hate it.

"Neither the things that are in the world." The second inflexible boundary builds on the first. Today there are more *"things"* in this *"world"* to *"love"* than at any other point in the existence of humanity. I am constantly tempted with pretty, shiny, innovative, imaginative, and enticing *"things."* They compel me to acquire and indulge, leaving me hungering, thirsting, and dreaming of more. Paul avoided loving *"things"* by detaching before he ever had a chance to attach— *"But what things were gain to me, those I counted loss for Christ" (Philippians 3:7).* Lord, help me to develop a holy detachment from *"the things that are in the*

world." I will *"seek those things which are above, where Christ sitteth on the right hand of God" (Colossians 3:1)*. I will detach by giving you the title deed of everything and everyone in my life.

Thought for the Day: A moment of indulgence can easily lead to a life-long attachment. The risk is too great.

Search Me, O God!

- The fruit of the Spirit is the ability to attach oneself to the right things.

- Ask the Holy Spirit to reveal to you any part of your life that excludes God.

- Take time to meditate on the phrase, "A moment of indulgence … a lifetime of attachment."

- How difficult is it for you to avoid, walk away from, remove, despise, and hate the world?

- Developing an unholy attachment is human; detaching from the unholy is divine.

- What have you not titled over to the Lord? What will it take for you to do so?

My "I" Problem with Not Loving the World
"If Any Man Love the World"
Day 43

"Love not the world, neither the things that are in the world. If any man love the world, the love of the Father is not in him. For all that is in the world, the lust of the flesh, the lust of the eyes, and the pride of life, is not of the Father, but is of the world."
(1 John 2:15-16)

"If any man love the world." I confess my hesitancy to rescind membership in the *"any man"* club. God has broken many of my worldly ties, but not all of them. I have refused to place some of my worldly affections on the altar. Their hypnotic trance is incredibly powerful, not to mention deceptive. It is imperative that I consciously remind myself that I am not of this world and it is not my friend (*John 15:19*). Father, make me so disgusted with the worldliness in my life that I readily fly to the shelter of the cross and seek cleansing.

"Love the world." What is this obsession I have with *"the world"*? It controls my thoughts, energizes my motivations, woos me with its promises, and dazzles me with its pretties. So, I look and listen to it. Before long, my lust transforms into living it. When this happens, I become a mindless slave to urges and indulgences that dishonor my Lord and ruin my pursuit of holiness.

"The love of the Father." My spirit pauses, as I reflect on *"the love of the Father."* These are words of compassion, comfort, conviction, and constraint. Paul wrote, *"The love of Christ constraineth us"* (*2 Corinthians 5:14a*). A conscious awareness of the Father's *"love"* for me keeps my natural affection for the *"world"* in check. So, I pause to reflect on my Father's *"love"* for me—a manger, a cross, a tomb; substitution, crucifixion, conviction— *"greater love hath no man than this"*!

"Is not in him." *"If any man love the world, the love of the Father is not in him."* I cannot escape the horror of these words. If I am infatuated with the *"world"* and *"the things that are this world,"* the Father's *"love"* is not in me. John adds, in the next chapter, *"But whoso hath this world's good, and seeth his brother have need, and shutteth up his bowels of compassion from him, how dwelleth the love of God in him?"* (*1 John 3:17*). These are uncomfortable verses for me, because they are too black and white. If I *"love"* the *"world,"* I do not have the *"love"* of

the God in my life. If I do not have the *"love"* of God in my life, I do not have God. It is impossible for the two to cohabitate. I choose God!

Thought for the Day: A conscious awareness of the Father's *"love"* for me keeps my natural affection for the *"world"* in check.

Search Me, O God!

- Why is it so difficult to remember that the world is not our friend?

- The three-fold process to becoming a slave to urges and indulgences are look, listen, and live.

- How does Christ's love hold you together?

- What does John mean when he says, "If any man love the world, the love of the Father is not in him"?

- What does it mean to not have the Father's love in you?

- How does one develop "conscious awareness"?

My "I" Problem with Not Loving the World
"All That Is in the World"
Day 44

"Love not the world, neither the things that are in the world. If any man love the world, the love of the Father is not in him. For all that is in the world, the lust of the flesh, the lust of the eyes, and the pride of life, is not of the Father, but is of the world."
(1 John 2:15-16)

*"**F**or all that is in the world."* John is about to reveal God's collective summary of the *"world"* in its current fallen condition. Everything that sets itself against God, entices me away from God, or simply excludes God from the equation of my life, fits into one of three categories: *"the lust of the flesh, the lust of the eyes, and the pride of life."*

"The lust of the flesh." This is the first category. *"Lust"* is a desire for the very thing God forbids and *"flesh"* seems to refer to the body. This kind of sin seeks pleasure, fulfills appetites, and indulges in passions that God strictly forbids. These fleshly lusts (i.e. gluttony, promiscuity, addictions, and laziness) appeal to my body's natural urges and obsessions. There is great momentary delight in their indulgences. At times, the cravings are so intense that I will do almost anything to satisfy them. Lord, may my heartbeat, my utmost desire, and my life obsession be for you alone.

"The lust of the eyes." The second category of worldliness focuses on passions aroused by sight. Chances are they would have remained dormant otherwise. It seems to me that this generation has more opportunities to awaken these passions than preceding generations. The media, Internet, television, and social tolerance relentlessly tempt me in ways I could never have imagined on my own. With one innocent click of the mouse, an Internet search arouses sensuality. With one click of the remote, channel surfing awakens my materialistic side. In an instant, potential *"lust"* becomes a reality. Father, *"lead* [me] *not into temptation, but deliver* [me] *from evil."*

"The pride of life." The final category strokes my ego. What is *"the pride of life"*? By *"life,"* John is referring to the things that sustain me. At first glance, I am tempted to boast in my strength, wisdom, income, and talents. My *"pride"* demands that everything and everyone, including God, be about me. It places me at the center of the universe instead of

God. It elevates me above the Master. Failing to submit to his will, questioning his promises, or doubting his faithfulness are examples of *"the pride of life."*

Thought for the Day: At times, the cravings are so intense that I will do almost anything to satisfy them. Lord, may my heartbeat, my utmost desire, and my life obsession be for you alone.

<u>Search Me, O God!</u>

- What entices you away from God?

- What "fleshly lusts" entice you? Is it gluttony, promiscuity, an addiction, or some other body passion?

- What awakens the "lust of the eyes" in your life?

- What robs you of complete dependency on God?

- May this last sentence be your sincere, heart-felt prayer.

My "I" Problem with Not Loving the World

"All That Is in the World"

Day 45

"Love not the world, neither the things that are in the world. If any man love the world, the love of the Father is not in him. For all that is in the world, the lust of the flesh, the lust of the eyes, and the pride of life, is not of the Father, but is of the world."

(1 John 2:15-16)

*"**Is** not of the Father, but is of the world."* It boils down to this. If it is *"of the Father,"* I must instantly attach myself to it. If it *"is of the world,"* I must make an immediate and complete detachment. When my spirit listens closely, I hear the Spirit's clear and uncompromising command, *"Wherefore come out from among them, and be ye separate, saith the Lord, and touch not the unclean thing; and I will receive you"* *(2 Corinthians 6:17)*.

"Is not of the Father." Herein is the holy standard by which everything is measured: "Is this of God?" However, I must confess that it is rather easy to put words in the Lord's mouth. God will never approve what he has already condemned; he will never justify what he has already damned. One of Isaiah's six *"woes"* against backslidden Israel was, *"Woe unto them that call evil good, and good evil; that put darkness for light, and light for darkness; that put bitter for sweet, and sweet for bitter!"* *(Isaiah 5:20)*. I cannot determine if something is or is not of God through my impressions, feelings, or logic. Discernment is dependent on knowledge of his written Word and the conviction of the Holy Spirit. If a thought, attitude, or behavior contradicts the Word, no matter how hard I reason, it cannot be of God. If I feel the need to justify myself, the thought, attitude, or behavior cannot be of God.

"But is of the world." Jesus explained to his disciples, *"I have chosen you out of the world"* *(John 15:19)*. What was true of the early disciples is true of his disciples in the last days. As a disciple of Christ, I find it imperative to have a clear and Spirit-directed discernment between what is *"of the Father"* and what *"is of the world."* Holy Spirit, grant me discernment and purify my heart.

The world is my enemy and I must detach my affections from it and attach them to my *"Father."* Standing before a great multitude, Jesus declared, *"No man can serve two masters: for either he will hate the* one, and love the other; or else he will hold to the one, and despise the other" (Matthew 6:24a).* With every choice I make, I give my heart to God or to the *"world."* Since, *"the world passeth away, and the lust thereof: but he that doeth the will of God abideth for ever" (1 John 2:17),* I choose God!

Thought for the Day: With every choice I make, I give my heart to God or to the *"world."* I choose God!

<u>Search Me, O God!</u>

- Is God's Spirit calling you away from an unholy attachment?

- Do not trust you impressions, feelings, or logic when attempting to evaluate if something is "of the Father." Rather, seek the mind of Christ.

- What does it mean to be *"chosen ... out of the world"*?

- Remember, with every choice you make, you give your heart to God or the world.

- "I choose God" needs to be our mantra!

Chapter 10

My "I" Problem
With Forgiving
Others

Day 46   "Your Heavenly Father"

Day 47   "For If Ye Forgive Men"

Day 48   "Father Will Also Forgive"

Day 49   "But If Ye Forgive Not Men"

Day 50   "Neither Will Your Father Forgive"

*"For if ye forgive men their trespasses, your heavenly
Father will also forgive you: But if ye forgive not men
their trespasses, neither will your Father
forgive your trespasses."*
(Matthew 6:14-15)

My "I" Problem with Forgiving Others
"All That Is in the World"
Day 46

*"For if ye forgive men their trespasses, your heavenly
Father will also forgive you: But if ye forgive not
men their trespasses, neither will your Father
forgive your trespasses."*
(Matthew 6:14-15)

To be honest, when Scripture brings up the subject of forgiveness, I become very uncomfortable. It's not that I am weighed down with grudges against others, nor is it that I have a bitter spirit, full of resentment and vengeance. The problem is that I never really know when I have actually forgiven someone. Is forgiveness a one-time event or do I have to forgive every time I remember the hurt or injustice? If I still remember the wrong done to me, dream about it, or find myself dwelling on it, have I actually forgiven them?

At the risk of being too authentic, I confess that I have a second problem with forgiveness outweighing any other. Jesus' message is very clear, and that disturbs me. If I forgive others, I will receive his forgiveness; if I refuse to forgive, he will refuse to forgive me. Now that is a very sobering and troubling thought. Though I often demand justice, I find little comfort in the equality principle found in forgiveness. I'd much rather be forgiven without having to forgive others. But, alas, such a desire is nothing short of wishful thinking.

Because forgiveness is such a difficult subject, I would do well to spend time focusing on my *"heavenly Father"* first.

"Father." "Daddy," the most personal and intimate name of God, seems to have been Jesus' favorite way to refer to Jehovah. Whether on the cross, in the garden, or with his disciples, *"Father"* freely flowed out of his heart with an unedited sense of familiarity.

"Heavenly Father." Though *"Father"* is a term of intimacy and privilege, *"Heavenly Father"* calls attention to his holiness, power, and authority. His ways are not my ways and he quickly follows his commands with empowering strength to obey. Though it is not in me to forgive, it is his very nature to do so. Further, because his nature dwells in me, I am endowed with the divine power to forgive as well. This is one of the most wonderful truths in all the Word of God. The thing God

requires is the thing he enables me to do. And, do it I can, if I draw from the power of his might.

"Your Heavenly Father." The word *"your"* is a precious word. He is not only *"Father,"* he is my *"Father!"*

Thought for the Day: This is one of the most wonderful truths in all the Word of God. The thing God requires is the thing he enables me to do.

Search Me, O God!

- Is forgiveness a one-time event or do I have to forgive every time I remember the hurt or injustice?

- Meditate on this: If I forgive others, I will receive his forgiveness; if I refuse, he will refuse me.

- Focusing on the Father is much more pleasant than focusing on the equality principle.

- How is your Father-child relationship with God?

- All believers have the supernatural ability to forgive.

- What God requires, God enables.

- Take time to appreciate the intimacy of your relationship with the Father.

My "I" Problem with Forgiving Others
"For If Ye Forgive Men"
Day 47

*"For if ye forgive men their trespasses, your heavenly
Father will also forgive you: But if ye forgive not
men their trespasses, neither will your Father
forgive your trespasses."
(Matthew 6:14-15)*

"For." *"For"* is Jesus' way of saying, "Let me explain why I prayed such strong and difficult words." Imagine the disciples' faces when Jesus taught them to pray, *"And forgive us our debts, as we forgive our debtors" (6:12)*. I can envision Peter leaning over to John and whispering, "Not sure I'm ready for that one." Although I'm not terribly excited about praying those words, I'm bright enough to know that simply disagreeing with God doesn't exempt me from his standards and expectations.

"Forgive." The word sends idealistic, unattainable shivers down my spine. It's hard to think of anything more unfair, more difficult, more challenging, and more maddening than offering forgiveness to someone who has intentionally harmed me. Everything in me cries out for fairness, vengeance, or at least a half-hearted apology. Yet, I cannot deny that genuine believers are primarily forgivers. At the foot of the cross is forgiveness.

"Ye Forgive." Surprisingly, forgiveness originally meant "divorce," "aphiemi." Divorce releases the offending partner from having to make things right. The offense is history, locked away in an unopenable book. It is the end, and makes room for a new beginning. Forgiveness is also an accounting term, rendering the balance zero and releasing the debtor from any obligation to repay. The offense may cross my mind, I may at times be tempted to dwell on it, and I may never have a close relationship with the offender again, but the person owes me nothing. What's more, I need to remind myself that it is completely illogical to revive something that no longer exists (the balance is zero). I have released them from their trespass and set my heart on God forgiving me of my own ill feelings and expectations.

"Forgive Men." Forgiveness, essentially, means I die to the right to repayment, bitterness, revenge, or hate. This is my holy duty, my heavenly calling, and the high mark of spirituality. Half-hearted forgiveness never impresses the Father. God-honoring forgiveness always comes from *"the heart" (Matthew 18:35)*. My heart is the depository of my

spiritual life, the authentic inner self, the "me" that will live throughout eternity. This is total and unqualified forgiveness.

Thought for the Day: Forgiveness, essentially, means I die to the right to repayment, bitterness, revenge, or hate.

<u>Search Me, O God!</u>

- Disagreeing with God doesn't exempt me.

- What do you think about the statement, "Genuine believers are primarily forgivers"?

- How does the concept of divorce affect your understanding of forgiveness?

- How does the concept of accounting affect your understanding of forgiveness?

- How do you know when you have forgiven from "the heart"?

- I must die to my right to not forgive.

My "I" Problem with Forgiving Others
"Father Will Also Forgive"
Day 48

*"For if ye forgive men their trespasses, your heavenly
Father will also forgive you: But if ye forgive not
men their trespasses, neither will your Father
forgive your trespasses."
(Matthew 6:14-15)*

"If Ye." Every *"if"* deserves a "then" of some kind (implied or actual). *"If"* I smash my finger with a hammer, "then" it will hurt. *"If"* I pay my electric bill, "then" the appliances will run. *"If"* I forgive, "then" my *"Father will also forgive* [me]." I want to scream at the top of my voice, "It's NOT that simple!" At this moment, *"if"* is the most intimidating, overwhelming, challenging word in this passage. Forgiveness seems almost a nonissue when compared to *"if." "If"* places the burden flat on my shoulders; it is my choice and mine alone. This little two-letter word keeps me in constant limbo, vacillating somewhere between justice and mercy.

"If." "If" seems to be a code word for my bitterness, resentment, desire for justice, sense of fairness, self-pity, hatred, and a host of sinful behaviors and thoughts. It is a deceitful evil, because it keeps the possibility of offering and receiving forgiveness in question. My righteous masquerade quickly gives way, revealing a desperately wicked heart, *"if"* I as much as consider the possibility of not forgiving. Lord, deliver me from the demon of *"if."*

"Father Will Also." This is the "then" consequence. *"If"* I *"forgive"* "then" forgiveness is available to me. Why would I not want God's forgiveness? Yet, as long as I am in limbo, I remain unforgiven. And, if I should die . . . .

"Forgive You." Three of the most astounding words from the mouth of Jesus are these: *"Father, forgive them."* Equally astounding is *"Thy sins are forgiven thee."* I cannot imagine a good reason for God to wipe my sin-slate clean, but thank God, he does. Father, my sins are many, most of which I did with full knowledge that I was rebelling against your will. Each time I convinced myself that rebelling seemed the better choice, though I confess that I had twinges of guilt along the way. I cannot begin to describe how disgusted I am with my wicked choices. Sometimes I minimized them; other times I rationalized them away; and every time I insulted your cross, your love, and my calling. I don't deserve your

forgiveness and feel unworthy to confess and receive it. Hell is what I deserve, but an eternity away from you is an unbearable thought. Today, I forgive those who have trespassed against me and I thank you for forgiving this unworthy sinner. Amen!

Thought for the Day: "If" I "forgive" "then" forgiveness is available to me. Why would I not want God's forgiveness?

Search Me, O God!

- "If" is an empowering term, for "if" forgiveness rests on my shoulders I do not have to wait for an apology to offer it.

- Is it a sin to consider not forgiving? What does such a consideration reveal about your heart?

- What is so important about holding a grudge that it is worth not receiving God's forgiveness?

- Listen as Jesus speaks to the Father on your behalf, "Father forgive (your name)."

- What do you think of this concept: If you feel you deserve to be forgiven, the chances are you have not repented and you will not be forgiven?

My "I" Problem with Forgiving Others
"But If Ye Forgive Not Men"
Day 49

*"For if ye forgive men their trespasses, your heavenly
Father will also forgive you: But if ye forgive not
men their trespasses, neither will your Father
forgive your trespasses."*
(Matthew 6:14-15)

"*But If Ye.***"** *Verse 14* started far more promising than *verse 15.* Both are
statements of consequence (*"if"* you do this "then" here is the expected
outcome). While *"for"* resonates with hope, anticipation, and empow-
erment, *"but"* is demoralizing, discouraging, and dreadful. The word
"but" is a hypnotic magnet, causing conviction from which I cannot
escape. I will linger by it for as long as it takes, while the Spirit ministers
the terrible consequence of an unforgiving heart to my troubled soul.

"*Ye.***"** Who do I think I am? What gives me the right to withhold forgiveness from others and the stupidity to refuse God's forgiveness? Do I
really think that not forgiving is worth not being forgiven? The fact is, I
<u>do</u> want God's forgiveness, and, at times, I <u>do not</u> want to forgive others.
I so badly want to rewrite these verses: "It mattereth not if ye forgive
men their trespasses, your heavenly Father will always forgive your trespasses." Now there's a verse—a verse from Hell—even so, many believe
it is God's way.

"*Forgive Not.***"** A few moments reflecting on these two words leave
me with a wrinkled brow, clinched teeth, insistent anger, extreme self-
pity, unmerciful hatred, and thoughts of revenge and getting even. The
revealing thing about this is, I wasn't thinking about a particular situation. The *"Forgive Not"* demon never travels alone. Some of his closest
companions, in addition to the ones already mentioned, are bitterness,
obsession, gossip, and a wide variety of "getting even" tactics (from
rumors to murder).

"*Men Their Trespasses.***"** Sometimes I forget that humans are human. I
don't expect them to be perfect, except when their lives intersect mine.
When this happens, I cast aside my "humans are human" philosophy and
immediately replace it with unrealistic expectations: "You must always
treat me fairly," "You will never lie to me," "You are required always be
on time," "You can never harm me in any way." Yet, offenses cannot be
avoided and, in many cases, abound. Humans will be human and sinners

will sin. Furthermore, when their humanity and sinfulness cross my path, forgiveness is my only God-honoring option.

Thought for the Day: The fact is, I <u>do</u> want God's forgiveness, and, at times, I <u>do not</u> want to forgive others. I so badly want to rewrite these verses."

Search Me, O God!

- What is the implication of "for" verses "but"?

- Do you believe this rewriting of verse 15 is the general attitude of most churchgoers? Has it been your approach to God's forgiveness?

- Take a few moments and reflect on how not forgiving effects you physically, mentally, emotionally, and spiritually

- If sinners are sinners, and saved sinners are sinners, shouldn't we expected to be sinned against? Shouldn't we prepare to have forgiving hearts?

- I do and I do not. Could any phrase better describe our sin-struggle?

My "I" Problem with Forgiving Others
"Neither Will Your Father Forgive"
Day 50

"For if ye forgive men their trespasses, your heavenly
Father will also forgive you: But if ye forgive not
men their trespasses, neither will your Father
forgive your trespasses."
(Matthew 6:14-15)

"Neither." The Greek language is poetic and powerful, often not following the rules of English grammar. *"Neither"* is one of those words. We could easily translate it "but not." *"But if ye forgive not men their trespasses, [but not] will your Father forgive your trespasses."* In other words, God responds to my *"but"* refusal to forgive with a stronger and harsher "but not" refusal to forgive me. Today, the conversation might go like this. I say, "But if I refuse to forgive others, God will still forgive me, right?" God replies, "Not!"

"Will Your Father." Talk about tough love! Unlike much of today's lopsided preaching that emphasizes mercy and overlooks judgment, God's forgiveness operates on an equality principle. He will do unto me as I have done unto others. God's equality principle saturates the pages of Scripture. When it comes to giving, Jesus says, *"Give, and it shall be given unto you" (Luke 6:38).* *"Judgment without mercy"* awaits those *"that hath showed not mercy,"* according to *James 2:13.* Likewise, the *"Father"* reserves forgiveness only for those who forgive.

"Trespasses." A "trespass" is a lapse of integrity, a momentary swaying from God's non-negotiable absolutes, or deviating from the mark of a Christian. *"Trespasses,"* on the other hand, is neither a momentary lapse nor a one-time deviation, but a string of lapses and deviations from God's standard. This is not one sin, but many. Sin breeds sin. The sin of not forgiving is often accompanied by the sins of revenge, bitterness, hatred, callousness, gossip, spiritual regression, anger, and evil thoughts—to name a few. The sin of adultery is the same. Adultery will often join forces with such sins as lust, deception, lies, rejection, a hard heart, neglect, resentment, and manipulation.

"Your Trespasses." Now it gets personal— *"your trespasses."* Since sin seldom travels alone, I cannot begin to imagine the vastness of sins for which I am accountable. They are my sins; I own every one of them. I cannot blame another nor can I transfer them to a different account. They are my sins and cannot be justified, avoided, or excused. If I do not

forgive, I will not receive forgiveness. If I do not show mercy, I will not receive mercy.

Thought for the Day: If I do not forgive, I will not receive forgiveness. If I do not show mercy, I will not receive mercy.

<u>Search Me, O God!</u>

- If you refuse to forgive others, will God still forgive you?

- Can you think of more Equality Principle verses?

- Care to list the trespasses (sins) you have the most difficult time avoiding?

- Not one sin will be excused by God unless it is covered in the blood of Jesus.

- Lord, may I honor you and offer forgiveness!

Breinigsville, PA USA
16 September 2009
224186BV00002B/2/P